Robert Alexander Watson

Gospels of Yesterday

Drummond, Spencer, Arnold. Third Edition

Robert Alexander Watson

Gospels of Yesterday
Drummond, Spencer, Arnold. Third Edition

ISBN/EAN: 9783744744515

Printed in Europe, USA, Canada, Australia, Japan

Cover: Foto ©Thomas Meinert / pixelio.de

More available books at **www.hansebooks.com**

GOSPELS OF YESTERDAY.

DRUMMOND : SPENCER : ARNOLD.

BY

ROBERT A. WATSON, M.A.

"Ah, what pitfalls are in that word Nature!"
                                    MATTHEW ARNOLD.

"Let us speak naturally and like philosophers."
                                    SIR THOMAS BROWNE.

Third Edition.

LONDON:
JAMES NISBET & CO., 21 BERNERS STREET.
MDCCCLXXXIX.

To write frankly on Christian topics without offending some Christians, or on scientific topics from a Christian point of view without earning the scorn of some scientists, is, one may say, an impossible task. The fate of those who still maintain that there is positive doctrine in Christianity and at the same time divine munificence, a real creed to be believed and contended for, a great gift freely bestowed on the world—the fate of all such is to run the gauntlet between derision and denunciation. One of these essays has already been called the work of an agnostic and the fruit of envy. Its appearance in a new form may only expose it to fresh condemnation of the same kind. As for the others, are they not wanting in courtesy towards men who are most courteous? But a critic is not always bound to speak under breath lest he should appear rude or incur derision. He may brave fate if he will, is bound to do so if it seems possible to advance even one point of truth against fatal error. Science and philosophy are just now in that irritable state which betrays secret doubt; and an attack on opinions may be more disturbing than one would imagine, because those who are committed to theories feel themselves on very thin ice which may yield anywhere. If this be so, however, it is neither improper nor unkind to them to use strong language; and, besides, they pose as guides. That they are all engaged, according to their own account, in leading people off the ice marks the irony of the situation.

It is only needful to say further that the first essay, the substance of which appeared in the *Contemporary Review*, is rewritten and expanded for this volume, and to thank the proprietors of the *British and Foreign Evangelical Review* for leave to reprint the last of the papers.

CONTENTS.

I. The Gospel of the Higher Biology—Henry Drummond 1

II. The Gospel of the Lower Biology—Herbert Spencer 61

   1. *A Millennium that must arrive* . . 65
      1. Good conduct means happiness . 71
      2. A chasm between life and life . 74
      3. The reign of *bonhomie* 80
      4. The social-organism delusion . . . 84
      5. Each man a species 92
      6. Are we stronger as we are happier? . . 101
      7. Thou shalt procrastinate 106
      8. How can an evolutionist predict? . 110
      9. The real law of pleasure-distribution . 114
      10. Has evolution been a mistake? . . 120
      11. Is Mr. Spencer a moralist? . . . 125

CONTENTS.

	PAGE
2. *The Reign of Habit*	127
1. Interpreting the more developed by the less developed	133
2. What does evolution command?	138
3. No ghost, no duty	143
4. The moral imperative of—*Gaster*	151
5. Man meddling with evolution	157
6. The mountain barrier	163
7. The deep of scientific doubt	171
III. THE GOSPEL OF NATURE—MATTHEW ARNOLD	179

THE GOSPEL OF THE HIGHER BIOLOGY.

HENRY DRUMMOND.

THE GOSPEL OF THE HIGHER BIOLOGY.

PERHAPS no book was ever received with more enthusiasm as a magnificent contribution to Christian apologetics than "Natural Law in the Spiritual World." Now that the excitement has a little cooled, and Mr. Drummond's reputation is secure, it occurs to an observer of religious phenomena to inquire what made the book so popular. And one reason is not hard to discover. There are numbers of people who find it almost impossible to keep any sort of Christian faith unless secular learning gives at least countenance to religion and enables them to feel that they are not altogether behind the age. To all these persons, on whose minds modern science had made a strong impression that it is indeed one of the eternal powers, there came the electrifying assurance that one who had been much in company of the scientific masters, had caught many of their phrases and not a little of their spirit, was as clear for Christianity as he was for science. It had been a question whether the evangelical belief could adapt itself to evolutionary doctrine—whether religion which "dares not leave science alone" could make every necessary adjustment to her demands. Scientific expositions were certain and authoritative; religious expositions had begun to seem archaic, faltering, inconclusive. When a man, speaking in the most graceful way and yet most dogmatically, with the air of a revealer and yet with something naïve and simple in his tone, a man conceding all to science yet making science prove the most rigid orthodoxy—when such a writer claimed their attention, how could they choose but hear? They had hoped rather than believed that Christianity could hold its own against Huxley, Spencer, and Haeckel. They had hoped rather than believed that Darwin and Spencer allowed them to go on thinking about a God. How great therefore was the delight, the comfort of finding a religious Tyndall full of evangelistic adaptations of scientific dogmas, making the most material laws prove to a demonstration the doctrines of the new birth and election to eternal life. There were indeed difficulties many and great all about the field of discussion; there were chasms and pitfalls many. But these were temporarily bridged over or skilfully evaded, and still religion and science kept company, the thoughts of one on every subject proving to be even as the thoughts of the other. Up to the moment when this book appeared they had shown mutual suspicion and dislike. To religion it seemed that science was her great rival for the inheritance of the ages; and science, weary of the persistent demands of religion, had dismissed her to the forest from which she came. How pleasant it was to find all this at an end—to find the two going arm in arm—religion discoursing in the most learned terms of modern biology, science quite taken up with the

THE HIGHER BIOLOGY. 5

discovery that religion was a well-meaning and docile companion.

And there was this further reason for the success of the book. Not for a long time had there been any notable contribution to the literature of religious mysticism; and there are many devout people always ready to hear one who gives a new setting to the eclectic quietism which makes the music of their lives. To them every kind of sectarian controversy is painful, and the bustle of philanthropy is uninviting. How Church creeds are to be reconciled with science they care little; nor are they troubled by the "penetrating gaze" which Mr. Drummond says science has fixed on "the back of phenomena." The quietist craves to dwell in the heart of spiritual secrets, to be absorbed in emotions which can never be explained, only felt, which take him far away from the hurrying activity of the age. Thus the remarkable fortune of the book we are considering was to be welcomed by those who were afraid of science, afraid lest its atheism should overcome their strict and definite creed; and welcomed no less by many who, having fallen away somewhat from the older and more poetical forms of mysticism, were ready to accept the fascinating novelty of "scientific" stillness.

Yet another element in the popularity of the volume may be noted. Believers in baptismal regeneration found in it a wonderful and timely support to their theory. While they were considering in their hearts how to avert the scientific condemnation of ecclesiastical miracle and sacramental efficacy, the new teacher appeared with an assurance that their conception of divine grace and its operation was in effect a scientific idea. He said nothing explicit—not a word of the priesthood, the orders and sacraments of the Church; but it was easy to see that his law of the new birth precisely corresponded with the doctrine of baptismal vivification. Did Mr. Drummond assert as a dogma of scientific religion that life must stoop from above to quicken the dead natural man? In the ordained priest they had one specially endowed with the life-giving power—definitely and truly a spiritual father. From the law of regeneration the book led on, step by step, to classification of men and the doctrine of a spiritual kingdom. In every step they followed it, and found themselves at last provided with a scientific definition of the Church, not much out of harmony with Catholic theology.

The book is a singular and strange production; it has had so far a singular and suggestive career.

Now there is no desire in this criticism to make light of the least attempt, earnestly gone about, to harmonise religion and science; of these there is surely a synthesis, and one day it shall be found. Nor is there meant to be any reproach cast upon the mystic, or upon the devout sacramentarian who does not share the pride of which the system is full. Christian mysticism on the one hand, the spiritual idea of the Church on the other—each of these has an attraction, a truth

THE HIGHER BIOLOGY.

of its own. Beside either of them scientific formulæ are pale and cold. The finest spirits will always lean to Augustine or Fénélon rather than to Paley or Baur; and a scientific interpretation of religion which still leaves room for the devout life is so exceptional that it could not fail to attract attention. It will be understood, then, that it is with reluctance we expose the real nature of Mr. Drummond's attempt to force religion into a scientific mould. He has written a fascinating and eloquent book; the style is charming, the analogies are ingenious and striking; an air of cogent reasoning pervades it, and a single reading leaves the impression that the basis sought for evangelical belief has been made good. In reality, so far from this being the case, the reasoning is fragmentary, and not seldom of the kind known as feminine; the chief conclusions are fitted to create scepticism rather than confirm faith. In a contribution to the *Expositor*, which is, so far, the only supplement to his book, Mr. Drummond says: "There is an intellectual covetousness abroad just now which is neither the fruit nor the friend of a scientific age—a haste to be wise, which, like the haste to be rich, leads men into speculation upon indifferent securities, and can only end in fallen fortunes."[1] This, we must say, is an apt characterisation of his own effort.

We discern a notion strongly asserting itself in Mr. Drummond's mind, that modern natural science is as

[1] *Expositor*, Jan. 1885, p. 39.

solid and true as nature itself. He seems to think that in this region of science human error and weakness have no place. "The doctrines of science, grounded in nature, are so certain," that beside them the truths of religion seem "strangely insecure. . . . The difficulty which men of science feel about religion is real and inevitable."[1] "The result of the modern systematic study of nature has been to raise up in our midst a body of truth with almost unique claims to acceptance. . . . The facts of science can be seen and handled: they are facts; they are nature itself. . . . Men feel that here at last they have something to believe in. . . . Now the mere presence of this body of truth, so solid, so transparent, so verifiable, immediately affects all else that lies in the field of knowledge. . . . Some things it scatters to the winds at once. They have been the birthright of mankind for ages it may be; their venerableness matters not, they must go. . . . Among other things which have been brought to this bar is Christianity."[2] Again, well on in his book, at a very critical point of the discussion, the author "hands over" a great difficulty to science. "The threshold of eternity is a place where many shadows meet. And the light of science here, where everything is so dark, is welcome a thousand times."[3] An imperious question confronts the student; increase of knowledge increaseth sorrow and darkness of mind, until at last he turns to nature, the echo which makes him sure of

---

[1] Nat. Law, Pref., p. xxi. [2] *Expositor*, Jan. 1885, p. 31.
[3] Nat. Law, p. 237.

a voice, and science—not philosophy, not revelation—gives the answer. "Science takes its place as the great expositor."[1] "Theology proceeds by asking science what it demands, and then borrows its instruments to carry out the improvements."[2]

A sober eulogy this; and it would appear to commit us thoroughly to what is called rationalism, or the Positive method. If every question arising in the whole breadth of human life and thought is to be tried at the bar of physical science, the position is the same as M. Comte's, that nothing is really known but what rests upon observed facts of nature; and where revelation is to find a place it is hard to see. Mr. Drummond is indeed vaguely persuaded that if Christianity can get time "to look up its credentials and adjust itself,"[3] it will maintain its doctrine of revelation and of Christ intact. The question, as he states it to himself, is this: "What contribution science has to bestow, what good gift the wise men are bringing now to lay at the feet of Christ."[4] But has he not given the wise men the right to judge Christ; has he not placed them above Christ? If scientific men decide, as in effect they have decided, that theology is an early and imperfect state of man's culture, that Christ was simply an Oriental mystic, and that the religious beliefs of to-day are mere survivals, what can one do who has given precedence to the naturalistic teacher and declared that science "can hear nothing of a great exception"?[5]

[1] Nat. Law, p. 31.   [2] *Expositor*, Jan. 1885, p. 32.
[3] Ibid. p. 31.   [4] Ibid. p. 30.   [5] Nat. Law, p. 18.

Mr. Drummond's concessions to physical science are extraordinary, and to the last degree rash ; the reverence he pays to it, placing it in the judgment-seat of the universe and clothing it in ermine, is wildly, fatally inconsistent not only with any just conception of things, but with his own uncompromising statements regarding the incapacity of the natural man, the barrier between his mind and spiritual truth, the great gulf fixed between the spiritual world and the world of natural activities. Why, the whole natural world as interpreted by the natural man—that is, science with all its facts and laws—is declared to be "a lower world hermetically sealed against all communication with a world above it,"[1] incapable of having any "intelligent acquaintance with its phenomena and laws." Pertinently enough he asks how that which only knows of chemical and physical laws can tell us about biology; and he asserts that, similarly, those in the organic kingdom—natural men—can know nothing of the spiritual world. We are to understand that "the barrier which separates kingdoms from one another restricts mind not less than matter."[2] It is "a scientific necessity" that the natural man cannot know the things of the Spirit. So we find not only a fatal concession, but a vast and glaring self-contradiction running through the whole scheme from beginning to end. The scientific man is the mentor of religious faith; with meek humility the Christian believer is to adapt himself, his Bible, and his Christ to the newest theories of

[1] Nat. Law, p. 76.   [2] Ibid. p. 77.

atoms and cells. Yet at the same time the believer lives in a state of fine superiority to this teacher of his, who exists as a mere physical product, his mind and body alike dead to God and to the whole spiritual region, who is incapable, although he dictates to theology, of knowing what theology is about. It is much the same as if the chimpanzee in the Zoological Gardens were promoted to a chair of moral philosophy, although we all agreed that it continued to be nothing but a chimpanzee.

The comfort Mr. Drummond's disciples feel in trusting him as a scientific guide must be rudely jarred by these discoveries; but they are only the first of a series. Take, for example, his claim to be an evolutionist, which requires to be made good if he is to reconcile religion and modern science. The "Doctrine of Evolution" he names as one of the instruments which science lends to religion. No quotations are more conspicuous in his book than those from Darwin, Huxley, Herbert Spencer, and others, who are nothing if they are not evolutionists; and in more than one section he traces the operation of law in terms meant to be such as are used by these writers. In speaking of religious backsliding, for instance, he builds up a definition by using the Spencerian ideas "balance, evolution, degeneration," and showing how they apply to facts of human life.

Now all this seems clear enough, but then at the very next step we find that the masters of science to whom our author professes to defer so humbly are followed only where his preconceived notions allow. For evolution is monistic, universal, opposed to catastrophe. The theory was invented to get rid of catastrophe; and as a doctrine it is now held, by Spencer and Haeckel at least, as the explanation of all change and all life everywhere in the universe, without cataclysm and without supernatural interference. These are some of the principles of monistic evolution as laid down by Haeckel: "The derivation of all organisms from some few simple original forms which have come into existence by spontaneous generation out of inorganic matter; the coherent course of the whole earth's history; the absence of violent cataclysmic revolutions; and in general the inconceivableness of any miracle, of any supernatural interference in the natural course of the development of matter."[1] Here the science, acknowledged to be authoritative, speaks. This is the law the enunciation of which is the boasted feat of modern science; and if that science be the true guide, as Mr. Drummond declares it to be, if religion "dare not leave it," then not a word can be said about catastrophe or divine intervention. But what does our author, who sends his readers to Spencer and Huxley for their mental outfit, grant when he desires to establish a spiritual kingdom? Why, that his theology does not proceed on the lines of organic evolution, that it "violates the primary principle of development; ... interposes a sudden and hopeless barrier between the natural and spiritual, and insists that the evolutionary process begin again at the beginning."[2] There is

[1] Haeckel's Hist. of Creation. London, 1876. Vol. i. p. 113.
[2] Nat. Law, p. 404. Compare pp. 406, 407.

THE HIGHER BIOLOGY. 13

also the daring assertion: "At this point, in fact, nature acts *per saltum.*" Thus the continuity of natural law in the spiritual world seems to be at an end. If, however, there is inconsistency, so much the worse for science. Mr. Drummond himself finally takes the lead, sets down the scientists he formerly lauded, and "enriches" the history of development with two catastrophes.[1] Let us take note how he adapts science in this way to support his theory, and what comes of it.

"Natural Law in the Spiritual World" sets out to prove that we have reached a time in which religious life and doctrine may become credible and attractive as they have never been, at least since the early days of Christianity. Let us get the idea of law introduced into our study of religious phenomena and they will fall into a great scheme, just as natural facts have fallen into scientific order. "Religious doctrines, many of them at least, have been up to this time all but as catastrophic as the old geology. They are not on the lines of nature as we have learned to decipher her."[2] Now, "if there is any foundation for theology, if the phenomena of the spiritual world are real, they ought in the nature of things to come into the sphere of law."[3] Let us then take for our guides through the spiritual world those laws by which our knowledge of nature "has been transformed into eternal truth," and "the same crystallising touch" will bring into science the facts of the spiritual kingdom.

[1] Nat. Law, p. 407.   [2] Ibid. p. 19.   [3] Ibid. p. 20.

Here we are at the great discovery which promises to make the spiritual world natural, and, what is of all but equal moment, to make the natural world spiritual.[1] "The natural laws are great lines running not only through the world, but, as we now know, through the universe, reducing it, like parallels of latitude, to intelligent order. In themselves ... they may have no more absolute existence than parallels of latitude; but they exist for us. They are drawn for us to understand the part by some hand that drew the whole. . . . Now the inquiry we propose to ourselves resolves itself into the simple question, Do these lines stop with what we call the natural sphere? Is it not possible that they may lead further? Is it probable that the Hand which ruled them (!) gave up the work where most of all they were required? Did that Hand divide the world into two, a cosmos and a chaos, the higher being the chaos? . . . This question, let it be carefully observed, applies to laws, not to phenomena. That the phenomena of the Spiritual World are in analogy with the phenomena of the Natural World requires no restatement."[2] "But the analogies of law are a totally different thing from the analogies of phenomena, and have a very different value. . . . And if the analogies of natural law can be extended to the Spiritual World, that whole region at once falls within the domain of science, and secures a basis as well as an illumination in the constitution and course of Nature."[3] Extending analogies is not quite the same thing as securing " a basis in the constitution of

[1] Nat. Law, p. 27.   [2] Ibid. p. 6.   [3] Ibid. p. 9.

THE HIGHER BIOLOGY.

Nature;" and even the illumination, as Mr. Drummond himself confesses in the next sentence, may be so wavering as to be of little use. He allows that in attempting to establish analogies one is apt to fall into gross error, and further he allows—a most important admission—that the value of likeness is quite different for different minds. But there is no need to be concerned about the difficulty of proving analogies or depending upon them. For, although our author uses the word frequently, it is not on analogy or mere interpretation that he goes in re-establishing religion. Here is the definite, unmistakable deliverance by which he must be criticised, which if he has not established, he has established nothing at all. "The position we have been led to take up is not that the spiritual laws are analogous to the natural laws, but that *they are the same laws*. It is not a question of analogy, but of *identity*. The natural laws are not the shadows or images of the spiritual. . . . As the law of continuity might well warn us, they do not stop with the visible and then give place to a new set of laws bearing a strong similitude to them. The laws of the invisible are the same laws, projections of the natural, not supernatural. Analogous phenomena are not the fruit of parallel laws, but of the same laws—laws which at one end, as it were, may be dealing with Matter, at the other end with Spirit."[1] This uncompromising paragraph ends with the remark: "As there will be some inconvenience in dispensing with the word analogy, we

[1] Nat. Law, p. 11.

shall continue occasionally to employ it. Those who apprehend the real relation will mentally substitute the larger term."

Very well. An eminently scientific guide-post on the way to the spiritual universe. The wise, the understanding, are to read "same" for "analogous" at the appropriate places. If others, less accomplished, do not quite know when to slip the first word over the second, that is not the professor's fault. We are assured that while "the spiritual world as it stands is full of perplexity," and "one can escape doubt only by escaping thought," we shall see clearly if we follow the new track; we shall discover that the spiritual world "is not a castle in the air, of an architecture unknown to earth or heaven, but a fair ordered realm, furnished with many familiar things, and ruled by well remembered laws."[1] Now we shall see nature "not a mere image or emblem of the spiritual," but "as a working model of the spiritual. In the spiritual world the same wheels revolve—but without the iron. The same figures flit across the stage, the same processes of growth go on, the same functions are discharged, the same biological laws prevail—only with a different quality of βίος."

It will be seen that we advance very definitely, very confidently. The law of continuity gives to these statements a justification which is to the author's mind "final." Wherever you trace a natural law, you may extend that law into the spiritual world; you may

[1] Nat. Law, p. 26. [2] Ibid. p. 27.

THE HIGHER BIOLOGY.

depend upon finding it at work throughout the unseen universe. There are not two sets of principles. If man is not to be "put to confusion" he must find "a divine veracity in nature." Therefore, as surely as science is science and God is true, as surely as we find the natural laws "continuous through the universe of matter and space," we shall find them "continuous through the universe of spirit."[1] Things are certainly made easy for us in a way we never expected. There remains in all the mazes of thought

> "No hinge nor loop
> To hang a doubt on."

Scepticism henceforth will be folly indeed, for we have only to learn the natural laws, their modes of operation, and the invisible will gradually become as real and familiar as our native place or the house we live in, as orderly as the world of minerals and plants. Let those who deny the position "furnish the disproof." To do so, they must "find a region where at last the principle of continuity fails;" they must "first overturn nature, then science, and last the human mind."

Begin then to enumerate the natural laws—gravitation, cohesion, impenetrability, inertia, electrical induction, diffusion of gases, radiation of heat, crystallisation, generation, development, integration, disintegration—how do these operate, and what conclusions regarding

[1] Nat. Law, pp. 40-42.

the unseen world may we expect to reach by extending them into it?

Gravitation? The Professor, strange to say, looks a trifle nonplussed. It would seem to be one of the first laws to track, one of the most likely and important. But when we ask him to show us gravitation at work in the spiritual world, he answers vaguely, first, that there is no proof it does not hold there; second, that it may hold, though it cannot be directly proved; and thirdly, if the spiritual be not material, it still cannot be said that gravitation ceases. It is not gravitation that ceases, it is matter.[1] The reply is given with an air of hesitation; and already, at this crucial point in the argument, there is an evident necessity to keep at a little distance from the inquirer. Gravitation is dropped, under cover of the ingenious remark that in the absence of anything to work upon the law waits invisibly—we suppose like Quentin Durward behind the sideboard ready to execute the king's will.

Plainly we shall have to begin our study by framing a new and startling conception of natural law; and now it is the pupil's turn to look bewildered; he feels as though he had followed a will-o'-the-wisp into the middle of a swamp. Did he not hear the instructor affirm that the law of continuity itself vouched for the rest as great parallel lines running straight from visible to invisible through the whole universe? Was he not commanded to believe that Nature might be trusted to light his way thus into the realm of spiritual

[1] Nat. Law, p. 42.

existence, and never leave him in confusion or uncertainty? Accepting the revelation, advancing as he was bidden, he is already in darkness. For the certainty held out there is nothing but a quagmire of *mays* and *ifs*. "Gravitation may hold on"—"if the spirit be material." To be sure; and many other things may be asserted after the same manner.

How many of the natural laws do visibly run through, or how few? An important question; and in answer to it there is a confession that when all the laws that have no opportunity of acting (for want of something to act upon) are eliminated, the laws of life alone can be distinctly traced into the spiritual world. The universal affirmation dwindles away to this: "The laws of the natural *life* must be those of the spiritual *life*."[1] Mr. Drummond does not admit in so many words that the biological laws alone are those to which he can make his principle apply. Almost immediately, however, we find every reference to others dropped. We hear indeed continually of a "Spiritual World" as a region in which there might be any number of phenomena besides those of life. It is a vast territory in which many of the old natural laws will find work to do; but somehow we never get the least idea of what goes on in it; we have no hint what relation it bears to the visible world, whether existing side by side with it or separate from it, under the conditions of space and time or beyond them. To use common terms, we do not get the least notion whether it is an ideal society,

[1] Nat. Law, p. 46.

or the Christian Church, or heaven, or something else still. It is assumed; it is talked of interminably; it is declared to be a theatre of many natural laws now known to us; but our knowledge of them does not in the least help us to a conception of that world, or the conditions under which its inhabitants live. To analyse the statements on this part of the subject would be wearisome and unprofitable, for they come to nothing. We are left with the hope that "the *theology* of the future will take off the mask and disclose to a waning scepticism the naturalness of the supernatural."

Now we shall find that the prop of Mr. Drummond's whole scheme is the "law of Biogenesis," and he introduces it to us as an example of those biological laws which order the spiritual world. But even as he introduces it he has again the air of knowing that there is a difficulty. "The *life* with which biogenesis deals in the natural world does not enter at all into the spiritual world. . . . The vital principle of the body is a different thing from the vital principle of the spiritual life." [1] Here, he confesses, the law of continuity " seems to be snapped." Yes, indeed; biogenesis deals with $\beta\iota os$, with cells, and germs, and material protoplasm; and as there are no cells and germs in the spiritual region, how can the law operate, and what is the use of it? The solution is amazing. To make this a difficulty is as rational " as if one were to say that the Fifth Proposition of the First Book of Euclid applies when

[1] Nat. Law, p. 45.

the figures are drawn with chalk upon a blackboard, but fails with regard to structures of wood or stone." [1]

On what kind of readers did Professor Drummond count? A person does not need much science to apprehend that from figures drawn upon a board to a "structure of wood or stone" is not quite the same transition as from life with cells and germs to life without cells and germs, from our visible tangible life to life which evades the microscope, "which is not ordinary vitality, not intellectual, not moral, but something beyond." [2] The audacious affirmation of a similarity, afterwards most pointedly denied, is however the sole support he has for the persistent claim that biogenesis is the fundamental law of spiritual life. And when he ventures to assert that, if biogenesis does not carry across, then there is no spiritual life,[3] he is still building on the extraordinary figment that spiritual life differs no more from the life of a plant than a wooden house from a figure on a wooden board.

We need not wonder that a writer who could get himself into such a difficulty as this did not see that the impossibility of saying more about the law of gravitation than that "it *may* hold for the spiritual sphere" is fatal to the projection of biological laws. If that is all he can say for gravitation, he has certainly no right to say any more for biogenesis. For it is under the law of gravitation that biogenesis works. All living forms are subject to the attraction of gravity; if there

[1] Nat. Law, p. 45.   [2] Ibid. p. 84.   [3] Ibid. p. 47.

were no such force there would be no physical life of the kind we know, for there could be no order admitting of life, no cells and accretion of cells building up an animal or vegetable organism. If gravitation ceases anywhere, there must be the end of biogenesis also.

Here the grand pretension utterly breaks down. We were to see the religion of Christ "placed upon a footing altogether unique;"[1] we were to find "amid all that is shifting one thing sure, one thing outside ourselves unbiassed, unprejudiced, one thing holding on its way eternally incorruptible and undefiled."[2] This thing is the reign of natural law in the spiritual sphere, "the identification of the laws of the spiritual world with the laws of nature;"[3] and behold! as we plant our feet the ground crumbles beneath us—the sure rock amid the tides of time is nothing but a may-be. That to which we have been led is not the identity of the laws—by no means. Identity is asserted and re-asserted in every variety of phrase that can make it emphatic. The quotations already given might be doubled without exhausting the statements of identity and continuity. What although we lose sight of the natural βίος; what although we lose sight of gravity; what although we come upon new laws which transcend and overwhelm the "older" (*older*, while the spiritual world was "first in the field"[4]), "we may lose sight of a substance, or of an energy, but it is an abuse

[1] Nat. Law, p. 83.   [2] Ibid. p. xxiii.
[3] Ibid. p. 52.   [4] Ibid. p. 53.

of language to talk of losing sight of laws."[1] Nevertheless there is not identity, only analogy, and that analogy based upon an unclosed inquiry.

Suppose, however, we agree for the nonce to call the quagmire solid ground, and to assume that it will bear; what sort of a spiritual universe is revealed to us? What does the Professor do with his "fundamental" law of biogenesis?

First, there is a survey of the controversy concerning the origin of life, an account of the Bastian experiments, and an emphatic assertion that scientific men have categorically decided against spontaneous generation. "So far as science can settle anything, this question is settled. The attempt to get the living out of the dead has failed. Spontaneous generation has had to be given up. And it is now recognised on every hand that life can only come from the touch of life."[2] He quotes Professor Huxley to the effect that the doctrine of life only from life is victorious along the whole line "at the present day." But Haeckel, as we have already seen, believes that all living forms have come by spontaneous generation out of inorganic matter; and Mr. Spencer has certainly not departed from his principle, involving spontaneous generation, that "there are not many metamorphoses similarly carried on, but a single metamorphosis universally progressing."[3] His law of the cosmos is the "continuous redistribution of matter and motion" under the same forces. To these philosophers, therefore, the

[1] Nat. Law, p. 49. [2] Ibid. p. 63. [3] First Principles, p. 546.

break between the inorganic and organic is only supposititious.

Well, Mr. Drummond affirms that "the passage from the mineral world to the plant or animal world is hermetically sealed on the mineral side. This inorganic world is staked off from the living world by barriers which have never yet been crossed from within. No change of substance . . . nor any form of energy can endow any single atom of the mineral world with the attribute of life."[1] "Biogenesis stands in the way of some forms of evolution with stern persistency." And the application of the law is immediate. "The world of natural men is staked off from the spiritual world by barriers which have never yet been crossed from within. No organic change, no modification of environment, no mental energy, no moral effort, no evolution of character, no progress of civilisation can endow any single human soul with the attribute of spiritual life. The spiritual world is guarded from the world next in order beneath it by a law of Biogenesis."[2]

We shall first look at this "great gulf fixed" between the natural life and the spiritual life, from the scientific standpoint. We shall allow meanwhile, for the purposes of argument, that experiments have disproved spontaneous generation—that there is "one incommunicable gulf" between minerals and organisms. Now science clearly defines the inorganic on the one side of that gulf and the organised on the other. On

[1] Nat. Law, p. 68. [2] Ibid. p. 71.

the one side there are earths, metals, gases, crystals, which have this characteristic, that they have no cells or cell growths, no protoplasm. On the other side there are plants and animals which even in their simplest forms have protoplasmic cells, and grow by means of the growth and fission of these cells. Science thus very clearly discriminates between the two kingdoms. Now if we are extending a natural law there ought to be a like discrimination, known to science, agreed on by scientific men everywhere, between the natural life on the one side and the spiritual life on the other side of a second great gulf. Science appealed to should be able to say, Here are the characteristics of the natural life, there again are the quite distinct characteristics of the spiritual life. Well, has science anything of this kind to say? Has it ever dreamed of placing men in two distinct kingdoms as strongly contrasted as the mineral and organic? To such an inquiry science, with a contemptuous smile for the ignorance of the question, replies that all men from the lowest barbarian upwards are to be classed in one kingdom. Of a race of men with some mysterious quality of being, or superposed faculties which divide them from the rest, so that a biologist would classify them apart, science knows nothing. Whatever then we come to now in the way of establishing such a race, separated by a grim chasm from all other men, science has no more to do with it than with the predictions of astrology or divination. What the truth about spiritual men is we are not here discussing, but only the dictum a scientific man would pronounce on the question of the second gulf.

Talking of gaps, there are, besides the first, two of which science does speak; one the interval between the unconscious and the conscious, the other that between the lower animals and man. Our knowledge does not as yet and may never enable us to bridge the chasm between inorganic and organic so as to affirm spontaneous generation as a fact. In like manner human research is not as yet, and may never be able to prove that there is continuity of development between unconscious organisms and conscious organisms, or between the lower animals with the anthropoid apes at their head and primitive man. Mr. James Sully, in his article on evolution in the *Encyclopædia Britannica*, asks if any physical theory can ever help us to understand the genesis of mind. He says that the dawn of the first confused shapeless feeling is as much a mystery as the genesis of a distinct sensation. Tyndall, in like manner, affirms that the chasm between the physical molecules and the facts of consciousness remains intellectually impassable. As to the division between the inferior animals and man it is marked in one way by the comparative weight of the brain, which ranges in man from $\frac{1}{20}$th to $\frac{1}{30}$th of the weight of the body, while in the gorilla it is $\frac{1}{100}$th. The anthropoid apes are separated from man by this decisive break, which no cave remains have done anything to lessen; and between animal and man there is a chasm of which the difference of brain volume gives only a hint.

THE HIGHER BIOLOGY. 27

Now Mr. Drummond has found it impossible to leave untouched the barrier between animal and man. He allows that philosophic students make it greater than that between the inorganic and the organic. But this barrier he crosses lightly. It "may be" a reality, it may make it necessary "to classify man in a separate kingdom;"[1] yet he betrays a strong desire, "in spite of" philosophy, and, we must add, in spite of the Bible, to get rid of the distinction between man and beast. With much daring he asserts that to allow it would make no difference as regards the general question. It is surprising to find one reasoning in this way who has insisted upon a gulf of his own, for which, as we have seen, science gives him no warrant. We would have expected him to see all the gaps he could, and make as much as possible of them, since in that way his law of catastrophe would be the better established. "Two barriers," he says, "are more easy to understand than one, and two mysteries than a single mystery."[2] Then, *a fortiori*, four must be easier to understand than two; and "the doctrine gains immeasurably by such an enlargement." Observe how the series would have run. First, a cleft between mineral and vegetable; second, a cleft between vegetable and animal; third, a division between inferior animal and man; fourth, between natural man and spiritual man. There would have been in this catastrophic division of kingdoms "a suggestion of the (new) evolution hypothesis too impressive to pass unnoticed."[3]

[1] Nat. Law, p. 409. [2] Ibid. p. 407. [3] Ibid. p. 400.

Now for what reason has Mr. Drummond selected from the gaps of which science is at present aware only one, and then created another of which science does not know? The reason lies in the exigency of the scheme, in the point which had to be proved. It was not desirable to have man in a kingdom by himself, for that would have involved discussing the meaning of the "breath of life" which God breathed into him. It was desirable to have chasms with something that might be called death on one side, and something that might be called life on the other. A beautiful symmetry was possible when it could be said, there is a gap between dead matter and living organisms; here is another gap, and it is between natural deadness and spiritual life. And what did it matter though man was classed along with snakes and molluscs, seaweed and lichens?—the scheme at least was perfect.

The author of "Natural Law in the Spiritual World," being aware that science fails him in his attempt to prove the spiritual kingdom, proceeds to found upon Scripture; not on the whole breadth of Scripture indeed, but on certain selected passages—a very bad habit not peculiar to him. Those passages, moreover, he brings forward, not to interpret them in the light of Catholic theology, or of Revelation as a whole, or of common use and experience, but entirely in view of his special theory and the great gulf which seems to be the all-important thing with him.

When Christ said, "That which is born of the flesh is flesh, and that which is born of the Spirit is spirit;"

when He said, " Except a man be born again he cannot see the kingdom of God ; . . . The wind bloweth where it listeth, and thou hearest the voice thereof, but knowest not whence it cometh and whither it goeth, so is every one that is born of the Spirit," did He mean that Nicodemus was utterly dead, as he stood there, to the whole spiritual world? What then did He mean when He said to the young ruler, "If thou wouldst enter into life, keep the commandments"? When John said, " He that hath the Son hath life, and he that hath not the Son of God hath not life," did he contradict his other statements, "That was the true Light which lighteth every man that cometh into the world," and, " Every one that loveth is begotten of God, and knoweth God "? If Paul wrote, " To be carnally minded is death, but to be spiritually minded is life," did he not also write immediately afterwards that " the earnest expectation of the creation waiteth for the revealing of the sons of God "? And again, did he not even say of those " who hold down the truth in unrighteousness," that the wrath of God is revealed against their unrighteousness, "*because* that which may be known of God is manifest in them ; for God manifested it unto them "? It would be impossible, one would think, to have more " impressive literalism " than this, and more explicit evidence that Professor Drummond has no right to drag the Apostle Paul into his service.

It is not within our scope, however, to compare texts with our author, or to show that for each one he brings forward to prove the stone-deadness of the natural man to all spiritual influence and truth, shutting him off from God, so that he cannot recognise God's existence—for every text that is wrested to support this notion there are whole chapters which most distinctly imply the opposite. In short, while Mr. Drummond has framed a doctrine of human inability the most uncompromising, the most rigid that ever occurred to the mind of man, utterly opposed to the omnipresence of the Holy Spirit, the conscience of right and wrong in man, and his responsibility to live according to a spiritual light which is never altogether wanting—of these doctrines the Bible is full.

"The attitude of the natural man with reference to the spiritual," we are informed, "is a subject on which the New Testament is pronounced. Not only in his relation to the spiritual man, but to the whole spiritual world, the natural man is regarded as *dead*. He is as a crystal to an organism. The natural world is to the spiritual as the inorganic to the organic."[1] Now a crystal is not expected to bear blossoms; it is never condemned for not bearing blossoms. So on the principle that man is no "exception to any of the laws of nature"[2] it is clear that he cannot think about his "soul," or recognise that he is sinful and deserving of divine judgment; and to condemn him for selfishness and unbelief and neglect of spiritual influences which he cannot cherish is incoherent and unjust. We are here at the very heart of our controversy with Professor Drummond. That science should be against

[1] Nat. Law, p. 75.   [2] Ibid. p. 99.

THE HIGHER BIOLOGY.

him becomes, at this point, a secondary matter. We accuse him of misrepresenting the teaching of Christ, of Paul, of John. We affirm that for the sake of his "mystical theory of the origin of life" he sets aside the great thoughts of all religion, of Hebrew religion in particular; he destroys the basis on which the law given from Sinai rested, on which the entreaties of the prophets were founded and their judgment of evil doing. For the Christ who came saying, "If ye were blind, ye should have no sin: but now ye say, We see; therefore your sin remaineth," fixing responsibility on men, and appealing to them as accountable, that is to say, spiritual beings, instead of this Christ we have one whose function it is simply to touch a man here and there in a mystical, miraculous way, and add something distinctly new to his nature of which there was not the least trace before. Of Christ the preacher of righteousness to men who are to be judged by the law of righteousness we hear nothing. When He complained of men, "Ye will not come to Me that ye might have life," He complained of those who, according to the theory, could not come, who could not hear, being dead. When He lashed hypocrisy, He condemned what was natural; it was as if He had denounced a leaf-insect for simulating a dry leaf, a viper for being a viper. To such a conclusion are we brought by Professor Drummond's attempt to prove that "the possessor of the carnal mind" is "dead to the voice of God," precisely as a plant is "dead to the voice of a bird."[1]

[1] Nat. Law, p. 159.

It is exceedingly painful to offer these criticisms on the writing of one whose work as an evangelist is so widely approved. But no one who realises the absolute duty in our day of upholding man's moral responsibility is at liberty to be silent when that idea is cast into the background. No doubt it is true that Mr. Drummond endeavours to mitigate the real effect of his chapters on biogenesis and death, and, as we shall afterwards see, attributes to man a good deal of what he had denied him. But yet again, as we proceed, we find that the theory of man's natural complete severance from God rules all the conclusions. The dogma is one that was never formulated before in the whole course of theological aberrations.

One other point still remains in the consideration of Mr. Drummond's theory from the scientific side. It is a quasi-biological theory. Well, accepting the conclusions of the latest biological research meanwhile, to what do they point us? Have they a word to say as to the origin of life? Nothing positive. It was not by spontaneous generation—that is all biogenesis asserts. Does it tell us about some vague life that at the beginning stooped down to the inanimate kingdom and took matter up into a new kingdom, and call that the origin of life in this world? No. Biogenesis tells us that where we see life *now* always a living germ or ovule must have previously existed. But how does our author apply this? He says that life of the spiritual kind is originated by the Living Spirit, the Breath of God, touching with the mystery of life the dead souls of men and bearing them "across the bridgeless gulf between the natural and the spiritual."[1] Now, assuming that in every case of regeneration the Spirit of God gives life of the spiritual kind to a being in whom there was no trace of it, no living germ of it, whose conscience and vague natural aspirations were not even to be called embryonic spiritual life—assuming this, the law of the change as affirmed is not biogenesis but creationism. There is declared to be communication of a life which was not in the organism before, the "infusion into the man of a new life, of a quality unlike anything else in Nature."[2] But in the organic world, where biogenesis rules, there is nothing parallel to this, at least within the ken of science. And when biogenesis is compelled by Mr. Drummond to reveal the origin of spiritual life, behold! we have not the equivalent of what is going on at present under biogenesis, but what by assumption took place in the beginning of organic life, at a period and in a way regarding which biology confesses complete ignorance.

What is biogenesis? So far as it affirms anything, it affirms the fact otherwise called reproduction. Offspring can only come into being under the law of biogenesis. Individuals multiply by the law of reproduction peculiar to their race. If there were a law of spiritual biogenesis, it would, on the other side, be a law of spiritual reproduction; that is to say, every one possessing spiritual life could reproduce it. And we may add, since natural life is fertile, spiritual life might be

[1] Nat. Law, p. 72.   [2] Ibid., p. 84.

expected to be much more fertile, wherever and in whomsoever it existed. Mr. Drummond so far confesses this. "The characteristics of life," he says, "according to physiology, are four in number—Assimilation, Waste, Reproduction, and Spontaneous Action. If an organism is found to exercise these functions, it is said to be alive."[1] Coming to this point, he attempts to escape by pleading that the investigation of function, merely as function, is very difficult. But the case before us requires no such investigation. The results should be in evidence. We are warned, however, not to look for results; and the reason must be that they would confute the whole notion of regeneration, which is not biogenesis, but creationism. The idea of the Christ-life is vainly brought in as a mystical escape from the inevitable scientific consequences of the position that natural law runs through the spiritual world. Mr. Drummond's Regeneration is in every case a miracle, and a miracle is certainly no law of Nature.

So much for Biogenesis. We come next to Degeneration. Degeneration of whom or what? The spiritual man cannot degenerate; he is lifted into correspondences which infallibly perfect him; he is bound to live, and the environment is bound to develop him. As for the natural man, he belongs to an order of things to which he is suited, of which he is necessarily a part. He cannot degenerate from the spiritual because he knows nothing about it, bears no relation to it.

[1] Nat. Law, p. 388.

THE HIGHER BIOLOGY. 35

With whom, then, does the chapter on Degeneration deal?

With man as man. "Why should man be an exception to any of the laws of Nature?" The secret of the chapter is that Mr. Drummond is bound by his theory on the one hand, and on the other is anxious to make up for his denial of responsibility to the natural man. So now we find that man can "neglect himself," can "change into a worse man and a lower man," that he can so neglect his mind that it will "inevitably atrophy," "inevitably relapse into barrenness and death." Being dead already, the natural man tends always, if he does not keep a stern watch over himself, to become deader: there is no other way of expressing it. "Without the smallest effort, . . . in the most natural way in the world, . . . the gravitation of sin sinks a man further and further from God and righteousness, and lands him," (he was never anything but dead), "by the sheer action of a natural law, in the hell of a neglected life."[1] In this there would no doubt be much force if it were stated rightly and on sound premises. But it is impossible to understand how the natural man can "feel within his soul a silent drifting motion impelling him downward with irresistible force,"[2] or how he is to check it, unhappy product of Nature that he is.

Leaving him for the present, however, let us see what proof is offered that the law of Reversion to Type is to be identified with this awful degeneration and uttermost ruin. A flock of tame pigeons, with their

[1] Nat. Law, p. 102.   [2] Ibid., p. 101.

varieties of form and marking, if turned loose in an uninhabited island, will revert to the original rock-dove type,—that is, *their descendants will*. A garden planted with strawberries and roses will, if neglected, run to waste. The strawberry will revert to the size of the wild fruit, the rose to the type of the wild rose. By what scientific right is this process called *degeneration?* Fantails, pouters, and other varieties of pigeons produced by breeding, are, scientifically speaking, monsters. The original dove is Nature's type, the type suited to climate and other conditions of environment—therefore to science the best type. Professor Drummond, talking as a "fancier" might, declares that the changes are "invariably to something worse"—"deterioration comes in and changes the plant to a worse plant, . . . the bird into an uglier bird." " If we neglect almost any of the domestic animals, they will rapidly revert to wild and worthless forms."[1] This is very complimentary to Nature; but what poet ever thought of the exquisite wild-rose-spray tossed against a June sky as "ugly," —a low deteriorated form? Where is the botanist who does not class the double flowers as monstrous? Where is the naturalist who will allow that the over-fed ox of the stall is a better, nobler animal than the *bos taurus* of the plain? Nevertheless, Mr. Drummond, as a scientist, assures us that change to the wild form is deterioration ; then, as a theologian, he applies the law. "The same thing exactly would happen in the case of you or me. If a man neglect his body, he will deterio-

[1] Nat. Law, p. 99.

rate into a bestial savage; if his mind, it will degenerate into imbecility and madness; if his conscience, it will run off into lawlessness and vice; if his soul, it must inevitably drop off in ruin and decay."[1] What! Do we here see the law of reversion to type at work? Do imbecility and madness mark Nature's type of man? Has the course of natural evolution raised man to the civilised state, and is the law of natural reversion to type irresistibly drawing him down to bestial savagery? Or is it all a mistake that man was made in the image of God, empowered to subdue the earth and to develop art, science, literature, government, advancing towards the ideal? Even so; the normal type of this greatest work of God is the poor Bastille prisoner, white-faced, trembling, idiotic. Nature is persistently at work, dragging him down to this her primary notion of him.

It is a singular position to take, that while evolution is the great law of races and of kingdoms, yet in each individual degeneration is naturally supreme, and a constant effort is required within or without to maintain balance, not to speak of progress. How did man, on Mr. Drummond's premises, ever attain a position from which degeneration is possible? Having this law at work within him, how can he have risen out of the animal? and how comes it that he tends to lawlessness and vice, imbecility and madness? That is not "the mere animal plane." But, somehow, he has risen, and can now revert. Nay, he was "lost

[1] Nat. Law, p. 99.

from the very first," and yet can revert. The race is kept in existence; it continues to subdue the forces of Nature; there is a constant straining of human law and human aspiration after righteousness, a constant effort to discover and apply truth; benevolence grows, the ideal rises, and yet to the spiritual kingdom this domain of man's hope and effort, man's art, science, and philosophy, is as a mouldering wall out of which a tree springs. The garden strawberry reverts to the wild type, the garden rose to the dog-rose, the fantail-pigeon to the rock-dove—all "worthless;" and so they find their "hell." In science this hell of the dog-rose and the rock-dove is simply a serviceable type, best adapted to natural conditions. Is that analogous to the hell of a lost life? Is it here that we find Nature and Divine judgment "squaring the accounts with sin?" Is man by the same law dragged into corruption, away from a God his carnal mind *cannot* love, and a righteousness of which, though his laws seek and his heart desires it, he is utterly incapable—as incapable as a flint?

The chapter on Degeneration would be sternly impressive were it only based on truth. As it is, every fresh sentence compels more horrified revolt from a use of natural fact which involves unnatural injustice. For how could man help degenerating if he were without the Spirit of God and left to the operation of a remorseless law? The pages in which we are told of neglect, and Nature "grimly humouring" the sinner, appear charged with Christian warning only to those who have taken no note of the reasoning—only to those who do not see that this Nature, which is said to "take her revenge" on the poor mole, on the crustacea of the Mammoth cave, on the man whom she made incapable of knowing God—this Nature is God's handiwork and instrument, framed by Him who sent Christ to seek and save the lost. But God, who made the worlds, "commendeth His love towards us, in that, while we were yet sinners, Christ died for us."

Before leaving degeneration we must observe that, as a natural law, it has nothing to do with death, nor does it mean ruin and uselessness. It is an evolutionary process, adapting a race of organisms to their environment; not that they may die, but that they may continue to live. By this law, regions which would otherwise have no life in them are supplied with vegetable and animal inhabitants; and in reality, every individual of a species known as degenerate may be struggling to improve itself as far as the conditions permit.

Mr. Drummond is weak on the subject of evolution as a whole, but he is strong on death. Death is his pet law. He sees death everywhere, and returns to it on every possible occasion. Biology having given the world "a scientific treatment of death,"[1] religion is now furnished with its necrology. We are all utterly mistaken in supposing that we are alive—that the universe teems with life. The important thing is not that plants, animals, men, energise and grow, but that all organisms are insensible, torpid, that is, dead to the

[1] Nat. Law, p. 143.

immense region beyond or above them. We are asked to fix our attention on the fact that the bird is dead to much of its environment and the tree to more. But besides that, "one cannot say it is natural for a plant to live. Examine its nature fully, and you have to admit that its natural tendency is to die. . . . Withdraw its temporary endowment for a moment and its true nature is revealed. Instead of overcoming Nature it is overcome. The very things which appeared to minister to its growth and beauty now turn against it and make it decay and die. . . . The very forces which we associate with life, when their true nature appears, are discovered to be really the ministers of death." Such is the position of the book. "This law, which is true for the whole plant world, is also valid for the animal and for man."[1]

True and valid for man!

> "And he, shall he,
> Who loved, who suffered countless ills,
> Who battled for the True, the Just,
> Be blown about the desert dust,
> Or seal'd within the iron hills?
> No more? A monster then, a dream,
> A discord."

And how does there come to be life at all? If it is natural to be dead, the rich variety of energy is mere disease. "Air is not life, but corruption," we are told. Sunlight and heat are equally "ministers of death." What is it that happens, then, when "the pastures are

[1] Nat. Law, p. 103.

clothed with flocks, and the valleys also are covered over with corn," when the great trees full of sap put forth their leaves, and man in victorious energy ranges over the world ? Are we henceforth to speak of all this as unnatural, a brief and casual interlude in the great Dance of Death ? There are those who thus speak, but they are usually known in the religious world as atheists and pessimists. Has there ever been in religious writing such an echo of Shelley's despairing lament—

> "Death is here, and death is there,
> Death is busy everywhere ; .
> All around, above, beneath,
> Within is death, and we are death."

Complete the circle. Let us be thorough ; let us face the truth. " One cannot say it is natural for a plant to live"—for an animal to live, for a man to live. Then the laws of life, of biology—biogenesis and the rest—are—what shall we say ?—laws of an unnatural state. Natural law in the spiritual world would mean that in the spiritual world also life is an interlude between deaths, the spiritual man an aberration, a monstrosity. So we come round to the great heresy of science, that consciousness is simply a disease of the organism, and at the same time to the Buddhist doctrine of Nirvana. If Christianity is to bring life and immortality to men it must have no dealings with this kind of science.

Now what about growth, that great law of life—growth which would appear quite unnecessary in the case of a spiritual man lifted miraculously out of the deadness in which he was born? Mr. Drummond declares, as we might expect, that it can only be an "automatic process." "The fruits of the spiritual man's character are not the produce of this climate, but exotics from a sunnier land."[1] "When the soul rises slowly above the world, pushing up its delicate virtues in the teeth of sin," the growth is described as utterly mysterious, due to the operation of an inward principle, with which he, as a man, has nothing to do. "The plant simply stands still, with its leaves spread out in unconscious prayer, and Nature lavishes upon it all bounties" that it needs.[2] So the one duty of the spiritual man is to be in his environment, "to abide in his conditions, to allow grace to play over him, to be still therein and know that this is God."[3]

The whole analogy between the Christian and the lily, which occupies the chapter on growth, worked out with much cleverness and fascination of style, is an exposition of the doctrine of stillness, otherwise religious automatism. Mr. Drummond complains that we "allow a miracle to the lily, but not to the man;"[4] that earnest souls will try to grow instead of simply having the miracle wrought in them. All the time he forgets that the plant has its struggle for existence, none the less arduous that it is unconscious, and, what is of more importance, that Christ's parable of the lily is directed against over-anxiety about *temporal* matters. It has positively nothing to do, one might say, with

[1] Nat. Law, p. 130. [2] Ibid., p. 138.
[3] Ibid., p. 139. Ibid., p. 131.

the principle of spiritual growth. Of what does Christ make the lily preach to us? It is that we are not to take thought unduly about raiment; but, on the contrary, we are to be concerned for righteousness, we are to seek first—make our grand object—the kingdom of God and His righteousness. Here much more might be said; the point, however, is clear. Our Lord did not use the lily as a type of man's spiritual growth, but as a symbol of freedom from worldly care. The development of spiritual character can be neither automatic nor unconscious; to promote it is the great care, the great labour of a man.

As to the contention running through the chapter on Conformity to Type, that there is "a bird-life which seizes upon the bird-germ and builds it up into a bird, the image of itself," a reptile-life, which " seizes on another germ and fashions it into a reptile," the embryos, as they meet the eye of science, being indistinguishable, that is to say, structurally alike, and the presiding life, as an operator, or artist, or potter, making all the difference—as to this ingenious allegory, we can only ask for scientific reference or proof. Haeckel tells us nothing about one potter being set apart to make all the dogs, another to make all the birds, another to make all the men. He says something, however, of the molecules, that is, the smallest particles of animated matter (atoms placed together in the most varied manner), of which the germ-cell is composed, to the nature and changes of which the subsequent development is due. As for Professor Huxley's "hidden artist working with his plan before him, striving with skilful manipulation to perfect his work," he has himself classed this kind of allegorising as only the "old notion of an Archæus governing and directing blind matter within each living body," and declared that "here, as elsewhere, matter and law have devoured spirit and spontaneity."[1] Does Mr. Drummond follow the scientist in this?

When we come to the spirit-life which is to fashion the spiritual organism, so that the imaginary law of bird-life building up birds may run on into the spiritual world, we are assured that the type-life is Christ. Such is the full interpretation of the text quoted early in the argument: "He that hath the Son hath life." The spiritual man is now an embryo. "*Can the embryo fashion itself?* Can the protoplasm conform itself to its type?"[2] No! "The old doctrine, severe, almost inhuman," is recovered by the biologist. "It stands to him on the solid ground of Nature. It has a reason in the laws of life which must resuscitate it and give it another lease of years. Bird-life makes the bird. Christ-life makes the Christian."[3] "Man has no power to move hand or foot to help himself towards Christ," says our author; that doctrine carried no conviction before, but now it has "scientific evidence."

Here, at an absolute dead-lock, Mr. Drummond dares to slip consciousness into the discussion in a single phrase, and in another to depart entirely from the doctrine so distinctly stated. "How is the Christian

---

[1] Lay Sermons and Addresses, 1870, p. 156.
[2] Nat. Law, p. 307.   [3] Ibid., p. 309.

THE HIGHER BIOLOGY. 45

to be conformed to the type, or, as we should now say, dealing with consciousness, to the ideal? . . . The type must be an ideal."[1] We might ask whether an embryo knows anything of the ideal, or needs to know. But we had better quote two or three of the statements which follow under this head. 1. "It is here that personal religion finds its most fatal obstacle." 2. "Men need only reflect on the automatic processes of the natural body to discover that this is the universal law of life. . . . In point of fact, is man not the veriest automaton?"[2] 3. In the nourishment of the body the initial act is man's. "Now whether there be an exact analogy between this . . . and the corresponding processes in the soul, we do not at present inquire. . . . Let man choose life. . . . This is our life, to pursue the type, to populate the world with it."[3] The facility with which the writer slides from one contradiction to another, from one conception of the spiritual life to another radically different, is something to wonder at. It seems to be all the same to him whether he talks about automatism or pursuit of the type—whether he declares that Christ alone can create the new man, or that Christians can "populate the world with the type." The difficulty of the subject is great, is enormous, but at least we should have had some attempt at coherency along the scientific line.

Glancing back: what definitions of *life* and *death* lay behind those pages in which it was said that the natural

[1] Nat. Law, p. 306. [2] Ibid., pp. 307, 308. [3] Ibid., p. 312.

man has a "soul," that he can "neglect salvation," and, if he does, will incur the "heavy sentences for violated laws," that "spiritual life is the sum-total of the functions which resist sin?"[1] We read that "the soul's atmosphere is the daily trial, circumstance, and temptation of the world." "It is spiritual life alone which gives the soul power to utilise temptation and trial, and without it they destroy the soul. How shall we escape if we refuse to exercise these functions—in other words, if we neglect the salvation of the soul?"

The writer has told us that the natural man has no soul-life, that he is farther from the spiritual than a stone from a plant, and cannot break through to it. And he has told us that the law of man's nature is degradation, that he is "impelled downward with irresistible force." Theology has, so far, been too modest, and it has been left to science to "pave the way for the reception of one of the most revolutionary doctrines of Christianity;"[2] the doctrine being, in plain biological terms, that man is dead because he has no correspondence as a natural man with the spiritual environment.[3] "We do not picture the possessor of the carnal mind as in any sense a monster; . . . the contention simply is that he is dead."[4] But all the time, it seems, there is a soul in this dead natural man, and the frightful affirmation is made that the atmosphere of the soul's life is fitted to corrupt. Of such a kind is the explanation, given in terms of science, of the state of man, the

[1] Nat. Law, pp. 104, 105.
[2] Ibid., p. 162.
[3] Ibid., p. 152.
[4] Ibid., p. 159.

Divine energy in Providence and the diffused influences of the Gospel. Then farther on we come to a description of the natural man as having a soul of which God is the "native air."[1] The Christian engages in a "superfluous task" when he endeavours "along physiological lines to find room for a soul,"[2] and "Nature and morality," we had been previously told, "provide all for virtue except the life to live it."[3] And yet the soul is "a living organism;"[4] it has a capacity for God; it is endowed with "spiritual senses" and experiences "spiritual hunger." "The chamber is not only ready to receive the new life, but the guest is expected, and till he comes is missed."[5] "Till then the soul longs and yearns, wastes, and pines, waving its tentacles piteously in the empty air, feeling after God, if so be it may find Him. This is not peculiar to the protoplasm of the Christian soul. . . . It is now agreed, as a mere question of anthropology, that the universal language of the human soul has always been, 'I perish with hunger.' . . . There is a grandeur in this cry from the depths which makes its very unhappiness sublime."

Now, is this *flesh*, born of the flesh? Has Mr. Drummond not found himself obliged by sheer force of facts to renounce, at least for the time, the mysterious law which "guarded the threshold of the spiritual world," which shut off that animal or crystal, the dead natural man, from all knowledge of the spiritual world

---

[1] Nat. Law, p. 274.   [2] Ibid., p. 226.   [3] Ibid., p. 168.
[4] Ibid., p. 239.   [5] Ibid., p. 300.

or relation to it? The descriptions here are enough to drive the reader into universalism. For who made this natural man? who gave him the longing and yearning which are yet only manifestations of death? How could He who gave the unregenerate man this desire for life refuse to fulfil the promise of that desire? Everything depends upon God. It is very strange, then, the natural man will say, that He does not lift us up by a life-force more potent than our death, that He will see so many of us withering, but never

> "Stoop to gather our life's rose
> And smile away our mortal to Divine?"

The truth is, although he never seems to perceive it, our writer applies the term *death* indiscriminately to inertness, imperfection, numbness, unconsciousness and disease. For example, in one place, his natural man is a person who has been poisoned and "only need neglect the antidote and he will die."[1] To be poisoned is not death, but disease,—a particularly unnatural state. When the limbs of a poisoned man are convulsed and all his functions are deranged, is he reverting to type? The analogy of poisoning is either true or false. If true, man in his natural state is not dead; he has life in him, does not need new life, but only a remedy. On the other hand, if the analogy of poisoning is false, which it must be on the general theory of the book, since you cannot poison that which is dead, then there is no wilful sin in us hindering the work of Divine

[1] Nat. Law, p. 109.

THE HIGHER BIOLOGY.   49

grace, and all we have heard and said about the Good Physician has been beside the mark.

In regard to parasitism and semi-parasitism, we shall only say that if Nature seems to be " for once at fault " in allowing parasites, yet they fulfil as best they can the primary law of evolution. The assertion that Nature " pours forth vials of wrath " on creatures that can " live merrily at the expense of others," and so lose nothing but rather gain in a practical sense, is a little puzzling when we try to make out what the vials of wrath are. Is it not true that the parasitic ivy outlives the oak? Is not the pagurus a very ingenious and thrifty animal, who deservedly prospers, seeing that he has had wit enough to anticipate the civilised human habit of using a house instead of carrying about a heavy carapace? With the application of this creature's wicked ways[1] we thoroughly agree; but we should like to know how it bears on the theory of spiritual automatism and scientific stillness. We should like also to know how any one can justify himself in publishing a theory of the religious life which will be adopted by the very people who are indisposed to think for themselves. Is not that to make parasites?

Much has been said of the impressiveness of the chapters on parasitism, and impressive they certainly are—very painfully so, for the most part. The very truth they contain is made perilous and offensive by the utter want of sympathy with the illiterate toil-worn multitudes, who have no choice in this life but to

[1] Nat. Law, p. 326.

receive from others, apostles of Christ or preachers of the Gospel, the truths they were sent forth to proclaim. If one of us is a parasite, we are all parasites. We have all adopted religious practices; it is to be hoped we have all accepted truths which we have not yet verified. Has Mr. Drummond discovered for himself, or even verified, all the scientific theories he uses in his book? To put the inquiry in a more pointed way would be cruel, although not more cruel than he has been to many.

Passing from this, which would require a great deal more treatment than it can have at present, a curious inquiry is suggested by what our author says concerning mimicry.

Inquirer. " There is mimicry in Nature, you tell us? "

"Yes, most surprising—insects like bits of moss-covered twig, like leaves and other objects."

"Quite so; and there are mimics in the religious world which correspond to these?"

"Mimicry is so prevalent as to appal one. It is difficult to know whether one is speaking to a dead natural man or to a saint. There are far more counterfeits than realities."

"Yes. Well, now, as to the insects, what do they simulate, did you say?"

"Oh, bits of twig, leaves—anything inert and useless to birds for food."

"Then the living insect simulates matter which may be described as dead. Is that so?"

"Yes."

"Then what is the parallel you draw? Does the spiritual man who is in danger for some reason, like the insect, simulate the dead natural man for safety? Is that it?"

"What?"

"Why, you see, the natural man is in no danger—is not living, and therefore neither has the need nor the ability to simulate anything—or what is it that he simulates? Is it death? No, surely; for it is the spiritual man that he mimics—at least I think you said so. This is rather difficult."

One might have expected that in proceeding with his argument Mr. Drummond would insist more on the doctrines of conscience and responsibility. When he speaks of the natural soul waving piteous tentacles towards God, it would seem quite impossible for him to pass on without a full treatment of Natural Religion, and some attempt to explain why the materials of natural character have "a peculiar qualification for being the protoplasm of the Christ-life." Explanation, however, there is none. All the talk about evolution goes for nothing. Evolution, in fact, is not wanted, and the Christian training and literature of these eighteen centuries are of no account. The author would say that they are of account in making the protoplasm more varied and responsive to the creative touch. But what advantage is there to the individual upon whom that touch never comes? History and Providence are stultified. A more rapid, more comprehensive miracle would have done all the work. Evolution has been allowed to drag humanity through a long course of pitiful experience which might just as well have been saved, for the Christ-life could have populated the spiritual world out of barbarous men quite as freely as out of civilised. There are passages scattered about the book which seem, especially on a casual reading, to invalidate much of this criticism and to make Mr. Drummond's position more rational, more Christian, than we have allowed it to be. But these are tentative remarks, from which we are carried as rapidly as possible back to the main contention; and when we reach the final chapter, it is thrust upon us anew, with even more emphasis than at first.

It is classification now. We are to see science defining the kingdoms, allotting to men their places on this side and on that side of the unfathomable gulf. "The distinctions drawn between men are commonly based on the outward appearance of goodness or badness, on the ground of moral beauty or moral deformity. Is this classification scientific?"[1] The position taken up by way of answer is, that as the man of science is concerned "not with the forms, but with the natures of things," as "no fundamental distinction in science depends upon beauty," as it is in terms of chemistry or biology we must have our definitions, there can be no escape from the conclusion that beauty of natural character has nothing to do with the distinction "between the Christian and the not-a-Christian."

[1] Nat. Law, p. 374.

THE HIGHER BIOLOGY. 53

A great deal is allowed to the natural man in respect of beauty. He may be like a sapphire or a diamond, exquisitely beautiful and perfect in kind. " The earthly mind may be of noble calibre, enriched by culture, high-toned, virtuous, and pure."[1] In fact, "moral beauty is the product of the natural man;"[2] it belongs to him as a special beauty belongs to the crystal. So far from depreciating the natural man here, Mr. Drummond seems to magnify him; but it is that he may insist on the error made by those who will find a connection between morality and religion. There may be no distinction outwardly between the natural and spiritual man. So far as those who know them best can judge, it would seem preposterous to rank the beauty of one with that of the crystal and the other with living growths. Yet of two characters, alike "pure and elevated, adorned with conspicuous virtues, stirred by lofty impulses, commanding a spontaneous admiration from all who look on them," one may be living and the other may be dead in the most rigid scientific sense. If the one has been made a spiritual man and the other is left in the moral region of the inorganic kingdom, then, "according to the law of biogenesis, they are separated from one another by the deepest line known to science;"[3] and the natural man, wherever he got his moral beauty, however he may desire and long for life, has none in him. "That which is mineral is mineral, that which is flesh is flesh, that which is spirit is spirit. . . . It is certain that the Founder of the Christian

[1] Nat. Law, p. 158.   [2] Ibid., p. 380.   [3] Ibid., p. 380.

religion intended this to be the keystone of Christianity."[1]

Here is the doctrine of Splendid Sins with a vengeance, and underneath it two valiant assumptions. The first is involved in the cunning use of the word "beauty;" the second, in the literal application of the word "flesh" to the natural man. Who gave our author the right to hinge everything on a question of beauty, which, as he truly says, does not make a scientific discrimination? Suppose we take righteousness, love, truth. The natural man seeking righteousness, loving mercy, ardent for truth, as he is pictured for us, may be beautiful; but that is not the point, that does not arrange him as a moral being. What does is the question whether there are two kinds of justice, two kinds of mercy, two distinct regions of pure and noble life. Is there a righteousness of the earth earthy, a mercy which does not drop as the gentle dew from heaven, but distils from the inorganic, a purity which is of the flesh? Mr. Drummond should go back to the Pauline epistles and read them afresh. Nothing can be clearer than their teaching, that as a man becomes pure he ceases to be carnal, and no longer has τὸ φρόνημα τῆς σαρκὸς which, by its very nature, is death. But Mr. Drummond's theory of classification has the inevitable effect of shutting up the Spirit of God into one region called the spiritual kingdom, and restricting his dealings to one class of men called Christians.

The author knows his difficulty, and faces it as well

[1] Nat. Law, p. 381.

as he can without giving up the scheme to which he has committed himself. He never indeed shows us how the spiritual life differs in respect of its beauty or value, its energy or fruitfulness, from the highest moral. He cannot declare that his unformed spiritual embryos are in this world able to exhibit the phenomena of life.[1] So he protests that it is unscientific and unjust to contrast the two. It seems almost to come to this, that the spiritual man may do what he likes, leaving it to the natural man to be moral, since the latter has nothing better that he can do. So great is the peril here—for there has been a heresy known as Antinomian—that the classifier, having hastily named the appropriate tests of life and declared that we ought to be able to detect symptoms of dawning vitality, has to get rid of the problem at last by "handing it over to physiology."[2] By all means hand over the problem. Be content, for the rest, to hint that scientific tests may be applied and may show the characteristics of an intangible life. The vaunted science, however, looks strangely like empiricism, a mere sticking of labels on specimens which, without the mark, could never be distinguished from each other. The operator stands among his cases classifying the subjects. If the gum sticks, the specimens are sorted; this one is "living," that one "dead."

One of the liberties taken by Professor Drummond is the use he makes of that majestic word, the Kingdom of God. In his speculations it stands opposed to the

[1] Nat. Law, p. 386.   [2] Ibid., p. 388.

inorganic and the animal kingdoms; but the true opposition is to the kingdom of darkness, of Satan, of human self-will. These have their contrast to the kingdom of God because they lie on the other side of the same sphere—the sphere of morals. *Inorganic, animal,* are not terms of this order at all. The kingdom of God against sand, clay, and metals! And the result of this juggling with scientific terms is seen when we come to the question: How may the new life deliver itself from the still persistent past? Strangely enough, the spiritual man is still inorganic; he still sins. How is he to cease doing so? Well, the easiest way, it is said, would be to die, as that would arrest all correspondence with the lower environment, and so he would shuffle off with the body, we suppose, all the defilement of matter. Unfortunately this way of escape is not at once permitted. The spiritual man is not, so soon as he is created, taken up "to heaven;" he must stay here and is "morally bound to accept the situation;" his business henceforth is to "die morally as much as he can,"[1] whatever that means. Truly a wonderful apotheosis.

Having thus made a complete separation between human history and Divine redemption; having made the appearance of Christ in this world quite unnecessary and His death on the cross a terrible enigma; having declared that "organic evolution, in spite of the vastness of its achievements, is simply a stupendous

[1] Nat. Law, pp. 180, 181.

cul de sac," and that "Nature's most finished product, man, is to the third kingdom not even a shapeless embryo,"[1] the Professor gives us the conclusion of his scientific gospel: "The outstanding characteristic of the new society is to be its selectness. 'Many are called,' said Christ, 'but few are chosen.' And when one recalls the conditions of membership" (what are they?) " and observes the lives and aspirations of average men, the force of the verdict becomes apparent. . . . The analogy of Nature upon this point is not less striking. . . . Here also many are called and few are chosen. The analogies from the waste of seed, of pollen, of human lives, are too familiar to be quoted. . . . A comprehensive view of the whole field of Nature discloses the fact that the circle of the chosen slowly contracts as we rise in the scale of being. . . . *Quantity decreases as quality increases.*"[2]

These italics are the author's own, and he proceeds: "If there is one thing more significant for religion than another, it is the majestic spectacle of the rise of kingdoms towards scarcer yet nobler forms, and simpler yet diviner ends."

The simple Divine end being the arbitrary culture of a few perfect white lilies upon a vast Serbonian bog of death. Worlds are butchered to make eternal holiday for a few favoured aristocrats, whose good fortune comes, without any condition whatever, in pure inexplicable caprice, from the hand of almighty Cæsar. It is to be presumed that he desires a few favourites to behold

[1] Nat. Law, p. 402.　　[2] Ibid., p. 412.

with him the cosmic gladiatorial show; still there is
a great deal of trouble for all the result. It would
surely have been cheaper and easier to create as many
peers as the court circle would comfortably accommodate,
without this unutterable groaning waste. True, the
show would then have been wanting, and the aristocracy,
with nothing in all eternity to do but admire their own
white-liliness of perfect pure " spirituality," might
have found immortality flat after a while. The arena
is necessary then; the pit of waste, the struggles, the
groans, the death, the black caves underneath where
the corpses rot, the constant rush into view of lithe,
agile creatures, shining, clashing, dying, and swept out
of sight again—it is all necessary to enhance the dainty
complacent security of those who have by mere caprice
been eliminated from the doomed mass and placed on
high—" automatically " saved.

No one imagines that Professor Drummond meant
to exceed the most notable performances of the "Hard
Church," or to supply scepticism with a fresh and
startling reason for throwing over Christianity. Perhaps he is not even yet aware that, outside the circle
of those who for one reason or another have applauded
his effort, there are many with loyalty to evangelical
religion as great as his own and with no less interest
in scientific research, who are sadly convinced that, so
far from helping the synthesis of Christianity and
Science, he has rather set them wider apart than they
were before. It would have been pleasant to allow him
success in relieving devout minds of the fear they had

of scientific terms and ideas, but that he has himself prevented. He has denied the very doctrines of science which he professed to accept. If on the whole, even with many faults of detail, he had reasserted with fresh emphasis and proof the cardinal truths of our holy religion; if he had found in the study of Nature one strong convincing interpretation of human life in its relation to God and eternity, the agreeable task of criticism would have been to follow his lines of thought and make them more fruitful.

As it is, to those who cannot feel sure of their own elevation and safety, or who have an infirmity of compassion for the wasted multitudes, the reign of law in the spiritual sphere traced by Mr. Drummond appears as cruel as it is unscientific. They are by no means "overcome with thankfulness that Nature is so like Revelation, and Revelation so like Nature." On the contrary, as they believe in God and reverence truth, as they trust to the working of the majestic laws which make no favourites and leave no waste, as they have faith in the evolution of Providence and Redemption, they will take leave to call the theory offered to them neither science nor theology, but a bastard Calvinism, with all the faults ever charged against the old, and none of its massive vigour or philosophic range.

For where is Christ in this religion? "The grace of God bringing salvation to all men" has a breadth and length and depth and height, of which the natural laws as here expounded know nothing; nor do they tell anything of the patience, and generosity, and cross of

Christ. Meaning to support religion, Mr. Drummond aimed at re-stating to a worldly and comfort-loving age the severity of the Divine laws and providing us with a philosophy of the new birth. Would to God he had succeeded! All that he has done has been to give us the alternative of pietism or despair. That is to say, if we accepted the book as a whole; but perhaps no one has done so.

THE GOSPEL OF THE LOWER BIOLOGY.

HERBERT SPENCER.

THE GOSPEL OF THE LOWER BIOLOGY.

THE most ardent disciple of Mr. Spencer could scarcely flatter him to the extent of saying that his great treatise on moral duty, "THE DATA OF ETHICS," is easy to understand. As a guide to holy living for the average man, it is sadly wanting in simplicity, fervour and other popular qualities. Compare it with the "Pilgrim's Progress," for instance, and very little can be said for the "Data" that would induce any perplexed soul to read it. Yet a person who sets out to regenerate society, or even strengthen the good habits of men, by means of a book, should at least aim at being read widely, and should not be much more difficult to follow than John Bunyan. Mr. Spencer can hardly believe that he is intelligible to the mass of people, and it is perhaps of little consequence that he should be. There are some, however, who read and are alarmed; there are some who do not read, yet are satisfied that he has superseded the Bible; there are some who read much and get more bewildered as they go on, vaguely supposing, nevertheless, that modern science must be all right somehow. Perhaps a few of these may be willing to follow an inquiry which shall use as little technical language as possible and will not be the least afraid of anything that is real science.

More than one line presents itself along which we might travel through the intricacies of the "Data of Ethics." The way chosen in these pages may seem rough and ready when compared with that of high philosophic criticism, but the design is to give some clear notion of this singular book, so that any plain reasonable person may judge how far the world is indebted to its author; and we shall take a short cut, so to speak, to the Spencerian Pisgah. We are led to believe that we shall find there a magnificent prospect, fair, serene, alluring.

The author of the "Data" is well aware that no scheme of life has any chance of acceptance with the multitude unless it offers a great hope, a vision of good times to come, and he therefore promises a Paradise to humanity—an earthly Paradise, which he sets in sharp contrast to the ignorant notions of Christianity. These have had their day, it appears; now in the fulness of time has come Mr. Spencer with the Synthetic Philosophy. Calm as he usually is, he can throw off the academic cloak in order to assault "British religion;" and, although he is strangely uncertain whether his moral scheme will ever become popular, he is persuaded that he alone has the true secret. The world has known dreams many and ideal republics many; at last the real is before us. Evolutionary science can speak of a new earth wherein dwelleth happiness; can place in our hands the Bible of the new age, a great Scripture of instruction and warning, persuading us to those habits that shall bring about millennial days.

I.

A MILLENNIUM THAT MUST ARRIVE.

We all know the present state of human society to be one of perpetual contest. Everywhere there are antagonisms and rivalries; individuals have to fight for their own hand, classes are organised in their own interests; we are all competing with each other for what is reckoned good, and many go down in the struggle. Now, in the Spencerian paradise there is to be none of this conflict. The arena of human life is to be cleared of all antagonism; the only tournament will be one of flowers.

"The relation at present familiar to us will be inverted; instead of each maintaining his own claims, others will maintain his claims for him; not indeed by active effort, which will be needless, but by passively resisting any undue yielding up of them."[1] "Though altruism of a social kind, lacking certain elements of parental altruism, can never attain the same level, yet it may be expected to attain a level . . . such that ministration to others' happiness will become a daily need."[2] "From the laws of life it must be concluded that unceasing social discipline will so mould human

[1] Data of Ethics, p. 252.   [2] Ibid., p. 243.

nature that eventually sympathetic pleasures will be spontaneously pursued to the fullest extent advantageous to each and all. . . . Gratifications must remain in a transfigured sense egoistic, yet they will not be egoistically pursued."[1] There will be "the achievement of gratification through sympathy with those gratifications of others which are mainly produced by their activities of all kinds successfully carried on."[2] Life having been facilitated to the greatest extent by exchange of services under agreement, "is to be further facilitated by exchange of services beyond agreement: the highest life being reached only when, besides helping to complete one another's lives by specified reciprocities of aid, men otherwise help to complete one another's lives."[3] So what we are to look for is a condition of things in which men and women shall all be healthy and active, busy and successful in tasks which suit them. The ambition of each will be gratified, and each will find pleasure in the activities and gratifications of others. Pain will then fall to a minimum; men shall be so prudent, so skilled in preventing disease, so able to fortify themselves against the hostile conditions and fatal energies of nature, that suffering of body and mind will almost disappear. And this is necessary, for "while pain prevails widely it is undesirable that each should participate much in the consciousness of others; but with an increasing predominance of pleasures, participation in others' consciousnesses be-

[1] Data, p. 250.   [2] Ibid., p. 255.   [3] Ibid., p. 149.

comes a gain of pleasure to all."[1] Men shall come to such a height of virtuous consideration for others that "though each, no longer needing to maintain his egoistic claims, will tend rather, when occasion offers, to surrender them, yet others similarly natured will not permit him in any large measure to do this; and that fulfilment of personal desires required for completion of his life will thus be secured to him : though not now egoistic in the ordinary sense, yet the effects of due egoism will be achieved."[2] Nor is that all: there will be so great a competition among men to please one another, that each, for the sake of giving his neighbours their share of doing good, will put restraint on his own good impulses; yea, he will be eager to place in the way of his neighbour such few chances as arise of getting pleasure by making others happy.

That is the evolutionary millennium " eventually " to come on this earth of ours. Slowly but surely we are moving towards it. Already " every one of the factors counted on to produce it may be traced in operation among men of the highest natures,"[2] and it is " irrational," " absurd," to doubt that it shall come. " Lack of faith in the evolution of humanity " is another of the " countless illustrations " of human stupidity. Every one who " leaves behind primitive dogmas and primitive ways of looking at things,"[3] who has scientific habits of thought, will be sure that the conclusion is " inevitable."

[1] Data, p. 255.   [2] Ibid., p. 256.   [3] Ibid., p. 185.

"'Courage,' he said, and pointed toward the land,
'This mounting wave will roll us shoreward soon.'
In the afternoon they came unto a land
In which it seemed always afternoon."

Fascinating and delightful is the prospect; but is there not a difficulty? Does the philosopher himself not see the difficulty? Mankind, he allows, "is daily forced by peremptory feelings to do the things which maintain life and avoid those which bring immediate death; . . . the result is, that in many cases pleasures are not connected with actions which must be performed, nor pains with actions which must be avoided, but contrariwise."[1] Surely this is so: and while man is man, and not some other kind of creature, living in another world than this, how can it cease to be so? The hopes our teacher has encouraged meet a rude shock so soon as we look straight at facts. For we have to live here amid the press and conflict of opposing forces, amid changes and sorrows, in the face of death, and how can we expect the pressure from without to be lessened so that we shall be quite free to study the finest shades of pleasure, and to seek at every turn the daintiest balance between our own and other people's self-love? Then as to the relations of men with each other, even though one did not find it necessary often to do that which is unpleasant to others, even though all the fools and knaves disappeared, yet human beings are so diverse in character, so incapable of understanding what makes happiness for each other, and, as life becomes more

[1] Data, p. 99.

complex, there are such increasing differences that a better state of things can be hoped for only if we may trust in some beneficent Power able to remove every evil without us and within us. Above all, we are compelled to ask whether the millennium here pictured can really be the climax of human courage and endeavour. Can those who glory in the heroisms of the past find anything alluring in a state of refined unbroken comfortableness? The Utopia painted for us appears to promise that, and that alone. Shall we not do well to turn from it and say: Let us have the toil and the struggle still; valour and endurance amid sorrow and pain are better than a paradise of egotism?

Setting aside these misgivings, we are, however, to follow Mr. Spencer in his demonstration. He would be the Columbus of this age. Sublimely confident in the drift-wood and tangle he has picked up, and his deductions from them, he invites us to sail with him to the new world. We, indeed, are in much doubt whether there is land in the direction he points, and whether, if there be, we should care to live upon it. Besides, he will have us renounce all else to go with him; we must sacrifice every other hope and scheme. That being the case, it is necessary to examine rigorously his facts and his logic. We will go with him if he convinces us. Blessed be the truth, however or by whomsoever discovered; but we must be sure of it before we consent to sell all that we have and take ship.

How is the millennial age of happiness to be reached?

Mr. Spencer's answer is, that it must, of necessity, come. Evolutionary forces are at work, and "the evolution of conduct continually tends" to the goal of "complete life."[1] As man has been evolved from inferior organisms, so will he be carried on through inevitable changes to the sure result. Among men there is a necessity of progress which, as militarism dies out, as individuals and societies realise their true well-being, must bring about the paradisaical state. Our emotions have their part to play; heredity preserves and transmits every improvement; social needs will press on each member of the advancing race; especially a great principle which has directed animal life from the first will compel men, both as individuals and communities, to such lines of conduct that there will emerge at last the perfect man in the perfect society. And what is this great and guiding principle? The conservation of pleasures. Let us acknowledge that, allow nothing to come between us and that, and all will be well; or rather, do what we may, this principle must control our life, we must be urged by it, and all must be well. It has never been clearly seen, and even now Mr. Spencer scarcely hopes to convince the majority; but, confessed or not, here is the law of our life, the one plain path of humanity; the "Data" takes no account of any other.

[1] Data, p. 98.

1. *Good Conduct means Happiness.*

We are accustomed to speak of good conduct. Whence comes the idea? In all animated beings, from the very lowest in the scale, or those next to the lowest, through all grades, there is traced a progressive ability to adapt actions to needs. Each action learned, each habit acquired, is continued only if it produces happiness. Actions tending to produce great happiness, protracted happiness, are highly evolved actions. As these fit the animal for a long and delightful life they are good, good in increasing degree, just as an umbrella is good which serves to keep off rain, and better as it keeps off the rain more effectively.[1] The functions of an animal are to be judged in the last resort by their usefulness to itself. Its life has no such relation to other lives that anything it does can be called good solely because it is advantageous to others. If a horse in a field rubs another horse the action is good, because the animal likes to do it, and expects to get rubbed in return. There are, no doubt, actions to which an animal is compelled. Care of offspring, for example, is necessary in order to the continuance of its race; and as higher ranges of life are reached helpfulness toward others of the same community is a condition of the safety and comfort of each.[2] Altruism, in fact, is so far "imperative." But always it is a creature's happiness that is the test of its actions. Through page after page, through chapter after chapter, dealing with molluscs,

[1] Data, p. 21. [2] Ibid., p. 209.

elephants, and men, the changes are rung on happiness, gratification, enjoyment, satisfaction, and pleasure. An animal may be complex, intelligent, sagacious; but these qualities are simply means to an end, and the end is enjoyment. Life has begun on the line of seeking happiness—happiness in getting food, getting more food, being able to eat and digest more food, being able to move about more quickly for the purpose of obtaining food; happiness in living securely, in living long, in producing offspring. Having begun on this line, on this line it must proceed.

When we come to human beings, we find Mr. Spencer allowing that "sundry influences—moral, theological, and political—conspire to make people disguise from themselves the truth" that "the good is universally the pleasurable."[1] But "cross-examination quickly compels every one to confess the true ultimate end" of conduct to be happiness. "The moralist who thinks this conduct intrinsically good and that intrinsically bad, if pushed home, has no choice but to fall back on their pleasure-giving and pain-giving effects."[2] "Every other proposed standard of conduct derives its authority from this standard. Whether perfection of nature is the assigned proper aim, or virtuousness of action, or rectitude of motive, . . . definition of the perfection, the virtue, the rectitude, inevitably brings us down to happiness experienced in some form, at some time, by some person, as the fundamental idea."[3] "The pursuit of individual happiness within those limits prescribed

---

[1] Data, p. 30. [2] Ibid., p. 31. [3] Ibid., p. 45.

by social conditions is the first requisite to the attainment of the greatest general happiness."[1] "Such egoism as preserves a vivacious mind in a vigorous body furthers the happiness of descendants, whose inherited constitutions make the labours of life easy and its pleasures keen; while, conversely, unhappiness is entailed on posterity by those who bequeath them constitutions injured by self-neglect."[2] But "egoism unqualified by altruism habitually fails."[3] He who would enjoy life as much as possible must think of others and gratify others. The pleasure of doing good to others "conduces to the physical prosperity of the ego" by raising the tide of life. A man's "egoistic satisfactions depend on those altruistic activities which enlist the sympathies of others."[4] In short, "conduciveness to happiness is the ultimate test of perfection in a man's nature."[5]

It is necessary to assume that life is worth living. "If it is held that there had better not have been any animate existence at all, and that the sooner it comes to an end the better," "then the conduct which prolongs it is to be blamed rather than praised."[6] But Mr. Spencer chooses to hold a "tacit optimism;" he goes coolly on his way in spite of all the pessimists; and his book, although it deals with æsthetic pleasures, and even declares justice or equalness necessary to happiness, is pervaded by a materialistic view of what makes the chief good for us. The bland conventional person,

[1] Data, p. 190. [2] Ibid., p. 198. [3] Ibid., p. 212.
[4] Ibid., p. 217. [5] Ibid., p. 34. [6] Ibid., p. 26, 27.

affable and well-off, is our nearest approach to his ideal man. When you come to one hitherto ranked among the highest specimens of humanity—Dante, Shakespeare, or, say, John Stuart Mill—the standard of judgment is still the same: Does he get happiness, plenty of it? Does he drink deep of the fountain? does he drink from it long? If so, he is a good man, he serves the end of his being; otherwise he is a failure. In fact, when the most highly evolved man is at last obliged to die his epitaph will be something like this:—He was good and great; he made his wives happy and had many children; he filled various comfortable offices to his own complete satisfaction; he bequeathed a sound constitution to his offspring, never had a day's illness, and lived one hundred and fifty years. He enjoyed good wine and good cigars in appropriate quantities, and had much delight in promoting the hilarity of his friends. He never bought a bad picture nor read a religious book. Now rest in peace, thou saint of the earth.

2. *A Chasm between Life and Life.*

Mr. Spencer holds it provable and rests everything on the demonstration "that there exists a primordial connection between pleasure-giving acts and continuance or increase of life, and, by implication, between pain-giving acts and decrease or loss of life."[1] He assumes that he has proved the evolution of sentient beings to be from first to last an affair of pleasure-seeking

[1] Data, p. 82.

THE LOWER BIOLOGY. 75

and pleasure-getting conduct. "Pleasures and pains," he says, "have all along guided the conduct by which life has been evolved and maintained."[1] We marvel to find such an affirmation as this in the same chapter which discusses the evolution of plants, for in that pleasures and pains have no part. It is anything but clear why, since vegetable evolution has advanced through innumerable stages without that guiding principle, no sooner does sentiency make its appearance than a new rule holds. If a species of plants can adopt a differentiation without having more pleasure, it seems strange that a species of animals should not do the same. One is inclined to think that there are habits of plants, formed without any gain of pleasure, quite as notable for their peculiarity and adaptation to circumstances as many of the habits of animals which are attributed to the guidance of pleasure. Why should there not be in the animal a continuance, even an increase, of the unconscious strain towards more organised life which distinguished the plants?

But, passing from this, we are to examine the alleged connection between pleasure and pain and the evolution of life in the animal kingdom. The few affirmations made by Mr. Spencer to support his contention that "pleasure-giving acts are life-sustaining acts," and that "pleasures and pains have all along guided the conduct by which life has been evolved," do not quite establish an evolutionary chain binding the lowest and the highest forms of life; for, if they did, it should be

[1] Data, p. 85.

clear that every stage in differentiation, everything making for greater complexity, has for its accompaniment increase of pleasure.

Now, so far as practical proof goes, there is nothing to rely upon. It would be absurd to affirm that research discovers anything which can be called evidence in the lives of existing animals: comparing one race of creatures with another, we have not even the elements of a conjecture as to the degrees of their happiness. Whether the sensations of a bee, are more pleasurable than those of a house-fly, whether an alligator is a more joyous creature than a salmon, are questions which must be left to the science of the future; as yet we dare not decide. The animal that has, say, ten muscles to move its leg, does it have more pleasure in moving the leg than another which has only three? Has a bird more pleasure in flying than a fish in swimming? Who shall judge?

Again, what reason is there to think that animals observe and remember minute changes of feeling as connected with new ways of using certain organs? It is often difficult or impossible even for human beings to discover what has been the precise cause of a particular pain or pleasure; and supposing the discovery is made, there may be, and often is, injury instead of benefit to the organism as a whole through some habit resulting from the discovery. It seems quite plain that among inferior animals observation is so limited, so frequently mistaken, that their evolution cannot be connected with the experience of happiness.

But it is in the transition from parents to offspring that differences usually occur, and here is more than a little rift in the theory. Who will show us the nexus of conscious enjoyment between one generation and another? Suppose a variety of sheep which have longer wool than their progenitors, are they aware of being more comfortable in winter than those which had lighter fleeces; and can they strike a balance between the comfort of winter and the discomfort of summer, so realising what evolution does for them? Are they conscious of an accumulation of happiness which may be transmitted to their progeny? Does the young baboon with a tail longer by one-sixteenth of an inch than any previous tail know himself distinctly a happier and better baboon than his respected sire or his venerated grandsire? If he does, where may the evidence be found?

Passing into the region of the human, we find no consciousness of pleasure common to father and son. There is an obvious standard of health, and we can judge pretty well how each individual approaches that; but there is no standard of happiness so that the experience of one may be accurately compared with another's. Supposing a father devotes himself to what gives him pleasure and transmits certain tendencies to his son, according to Mr. Spencer, the son, participating in the father's nature, ought to take over his happiness, and so " raise the aggregate happiness of the species."[1] In point of fact, however, the son may cordially detest

[1] Data, p. 190.

his father's gratifications and find himself continually thwarted in his own pursuit of enjoyment by the inclinations he has inherited. There is a familiar story of a military man, the son of an eminent novelist, who never read his father's works and was bored by hearing about them. In numberless instances drunken parents transmit to their children tendencies which are a continual torment and danger. The pleasure of the father becomes the curse of the son. Children are constantly repudiating the way of life in which they would find the kind of pleasure heredity predisposes them to enjoy. The father is a hunting squire, the son is a plodding mathematician. The mother is a society lady, the daughter a bookish recluse. In short, each life finds its own consciousness, goes forward on its own impulse, rests upon its own experience.

How we begin to act is determined for us by heredity chiefly; that sets us to accept one motive rather than another, to take a certain line. Soon, however, there awakes the consciousness of the *ego*, and with it personal activity, which gains strength and makes a distinct path of its own. The *ego* with heredity always working in it and through it gathers from the environment on its own account, and the hereditary strain may be felt as a hindrance. The development of consciousness separates the individual quite as much from progenitors as from companions. The life becomes unique. So between individual and individual, that is to say, between consciousness and consciousness, there is a chasm much too wide to be crossed by community of feeling, so that evolutionary progress may be an affair of happiness. No doubt there are musical families and mathematical families, in which the strain continues for generations. But within these families, along with a measure of resemblance, there may be the widest varieties of taste and character; pleasure may be pursued, in spite of the point of similarity, along divergent lines.

Here, then, we have a first grave difficulty in accepting the hope of Mr. Spencer's millennium. If it depends on the conservation of pleasures from age to age, pleasures that are invariably connected with more and fuller life, if it is this principle that is to guide the generations towards the goal, no certainty whatever can be found for the expectation of progress. Granting a certain rough capacity which the human race evidently possesses for keeping hold of improvements that are directly useful and add distinctly to comfort, such as having water and gas distributed through a town and supplied to every house, having systems of railways and telegraphs and the post-office, when we come to those finer pleasures which in the "Data of Ethics" are counted on for the future progress of our race, there is no certainty that they will be valued beyond the present generation. The fathers may be for peace, the sons may be for revolution and war. The fathers and mothers may be for a kind of life which the old-fashioned family doctor regulates—precise, steady-going, temperate—the sons and daughters may declare for adventure and Bohemianism.

We, of course, admit that amongst lower animals

there has been a conservative principle at work, and that, partly as a result of it, they have certain aptitudes and pleasures. But there are many grounds for believing that in their case the conservative principle tends as much to keep down as to increase the sum of happiness. Amongst the birds, for instance, how comes it that, whilst swallows and cuckoos travel south before winter, so many species, not a whit more robust, have never acquired the habit of migration, and remain in an uncongenial climate to be decimated, sometimes almost exterminated by frost and starvation?

But among men, while the conservative principle operates often against increase of pleasure, whilst old-fashioned ways of treating disease, old notions of comfort and duty, strangely foolish as we think, die out slowly, on the other hand there is an aptness to seek new methods of life, new kinds of activity, which may or may not bring pleasure, a restiveness that makes orderly evolution quite problematical.

3. *The Reign of Bonhomie.*

Proceeding to another condition of evolutionary progress on which great stress is laid, we shall find difficulties quite as great, if not greater. Our species, we are told, "is distinguished as having a formula for complete life which specially recognises the relations of each individual to others in presence of whom and in co-operation with whom he has to live."[1] If there is

[1] Data, p. 133.

to be a happy society composed of happy individuals there must be "identification of personal advantage with the advantage of fellow-citizens."[1] Our author teaches that evolution directly and steadily promotes other-regarding actions as the means of obtaining complete enjoyment for self and that it will thereby perfect all social conditions. We are to trace the process.

The first stage in the development of altruism is care for offspring. Then there is attention to the wishes of kindred and of immediate friends. So the circle of interest and sympathy widens, each finding it his own gain to consider the well-being of others. There has been an advance from family altruism to a measure of social altruism, and there will be progress on this line. If we are not altruistic enough to prevent disease, so far as we can, from attacking others,[2] we are ourselves exposed to more risk. If we are not altruistic enough to see that farming folk are educated our food will be dear. If we do not take trouble in the training of boys they will make bad inefficient workmen. It is marvellous, too, we are told, how it should ever have been said that "the conditions to success are a hard heart and a sound digestion, considering the many proofs that success even of a material kind, greatly depending as it does on the good offices of others, is furthered by whatever creates goodwill in others." We must beget friendship by friendliness if we are to prosper. Further, if we are good-natured toward others, even without any expectation of reward, we

---

[1] Data, p. 208.   [2] Ibid., p. 209 et seq.

shall kindle their attachment, and they will show "unstinted benevolence" toward us.[1] Again, "function entails waste," and you must rest sometimes from selfish pleasures in order that, after making others happy, you may return refreshed by altruism to your personal enjoyment. In fact, you have but to care for yourself wisely and you will gradually be led to perfect sympathy with others, embracing all your fellow-creatures in extensive arms of philanthropy. All this will come naturally, without anything that can properly be called self-sacrifice—which indeed is odious—if we only submit ourselves to the law of evolution.

What a charming prospect is here! What a pity it is that we cannot abandon ourselves to it! But although Mr. Spencer has forgotten certain facts of human nature which hinder the general reign of *bonhomie*, they present themselves to the mind of the critic very persistently. Are not the most of people somewhat parochial in their benevolence, apt rather to restrict than to extend their generosity, not to consider all, but only the few immediately connected with them? It would be interesting to follow this inquiry with the view of discovering how far, apart from Christianity, there is any reason for the hope we are invited to cherish. But we must leave this question, like so many that emerge in the discussion, and pass to another which has more point. Has Mr. Spencer entirely forgotten the immense power which antipathies have in the government of human life? Where, in all his fine

[1] Data, p. 212.

account of morals, politics, and society, is the evolution of hatreds, jealousies, rivalries and the causes of them, which are diverse and innumerable? Is evolution sifting out all these feelings and leaving only the good grain which shall yield a harvest of judicious altruism? Well, in the first place, we cannot see that anything of the kind is at present going on. National rivalries are still very intense, the repulsions between classes of society are still very strong; there are literary, artistic, theological oppositions, all of which breed jealousies and separations quite as deep as they used to be, though less visible. That men can dine together while they detest each other is every now and then proved by some biography which is popular because of its "revelations."

And then, in the second place, it must be observed that antipathies produce a kind of happiness. This may be exceedingly awkward for the Spencerian theory, but it is nevertheless true. Not to speak here of righteous indignation, which is a vital activity of the highest kind, not to dwell upon the fact that any man who has thought about life to purpose is bound to cherish many antipathies, could not otherwise complete himself, it must be allowed that petty rivalries and dislikes are often a source of gratification. What delight some men find in prognosticating the defeat of a rival, in watching for it, in comparing their own wisdom with his folly! what comfort in feeling that when he finally fails he has quite deserved to do so! Will Mr. Spencer deny that the evolutionary philosopher has pleasure in exposing the stupidity of Christians and the aggravating smartness of Socialists? Is there not anger in celestial minds, and is it not a stimulating emotion? May we not predict, since prediction is lawful, that the happiness of hating and circumventing and overturning others, which has already established itself in the course of evolution, will keep its place amongst natural men, side by side with the genial altruism which appears too easy-going to aid vitality in any marked degree?

The whole picture of social evolution given in the "Data of Ethics" is a kind of study in rose-colour, done on prepared card-board. But in broad day neither lights nor shadows are rose-coloured. And unless mere conservation of pleasures can be warranted to change the brute into a gracious and generous gentleman, unless mere sentimentalism will ensure that the rival in a woman's affection shall be loved like a brother, unless we have something else to depend upon than natural altruism, the millennium of happiness must needs appear as far off, nay further than when bees began to live together in colonies, allowing Mr. Spencer the benefit of the fact that even they are not altruistic enough to go on feeding the drones when supplies run short.

4. *The Social Organism Delusion.*

What has been said in criticism of the attempt to make moral evolution an affair of happiness is emphasised when we pass to consider Mr. Spencer's doctrine of the social organism, a doctrine which, for various reasons, he must by this time wish he had never invented. If, in our summary of it, there should seem to be incoherence, the reason lies in the difficulty of bringing his various statements into harmony. He tells us that "a nation of human beings may be truly regarded as an organism. . . . Though discrete instead of concrete, the social aggregate is a living whole."[1] But, as all the units possess the capacity for happiness and misery, "it results that the welfare of the aggregate apart from that of the units is not an end to be sought: the society exists for the benefit of its members, not its members for the benefit of the society." Drawing a parallel between the social organism and the body of an animal, he shows how in each there is continuous growth of the whole, how the parts become unlike and assume unlike activities, how there is reciprocal aid and mutual dependence among the parts, how a rising manufacturing town like Barrow corresponds to an incipient liver, and the roads connecting the town with other towns correspond to the biliary ducts and hepatic bloodvessels. Thus we have a universal law of organic evolution; and in the "Data of Ethics" it is applied to moralisation. "There is a supposable formula for the activities of each species" of animals which would give a system of morality for that species. Such a system, however, " would have little or no reference to the welfare of others than self and offspring."[2] But when we ascend from beings of lower kinds to man, and especially civilised man, the

[1] Principles of Sociology, p. 473 et seq.
[2] Data, p. 132 et seq.

formula for his complete life "specially recognises the relations of each individual to others in presence of whom, and in co-operation with whom, he has to live. . . . From the sociological point of view, ethics becomes nothing else than a definite account of the forms of conduct that are fitted to the associated state"—the social organism—"in such wise that the lives of each and all may be the greatest possible, alike in length and breadth."[1] "A society is conceivable formed of men leading perfectly inoffensive lives, scrupulously fulfilling their contracts and efficiently rearing their offspring, who yet, yielding to one another no advantages beyond those agreed upon, fall short of that highest degree of life which the gratuitous rendering of services makes possible."[2] But the law of evolution is sure to bring those who constitute a society into a higher state of happiness. That they can make each other happy by beneficence implies that they will, and the sociological view of ethics discloses the conditions "under which alone associated activities can be so carried on that the complete living of each consists with, and conduces to, the complete living of all."

Now, we have found one difficulty in accepting the statement that "the social organism is a living whole," in any respect like an animal—this, namely, that the evolution of animal life is declared by Mr. Spencer to depend on the consciousness of happiness. The social organism has no consciousness either of pain or pleasure; —it is the units, and the units alone, that feel happy or

[1] Data, p. 133. [2] Ibid., p. 147.

THE LOWER BIOLOGY. 87

miserable. How, then, can a society be declared to live and to evolve after the manner of an organism? And besides, although it is by storing up the enjoyments of individuals that evolution is supposed to advance, yet for a long period in the history of every society, as Mr. Spencer himself allows, the life of the organism "must rank above the life of the units." He has pronounced "the welfare of the aggregate apart from that of the units not an end to be sought;" the happiness of the individual is the main thing, "the ultimate end." And yet, in the evolution of civilised man, the social organism which is necessary to the perfect life of the individual cannot be evolved without making the demand on those who compose it that they neglect their own happiness for its sake. Mr. Spencer confines this difficulty to the militant stage of society, when one community is in danger of being broken up by the attacks of others. Limiting the problem in that way, making no attempt to square the facts with personal or family pleasure-seeking, he lightly passes on to the industrial stage, in which he rashly says no sacrifices are demanded in the name of society. Here, however, we should think, most people will differ from him entirely. So far as we can see, a society devoted to industry will always have to demand sacrifices of many of its members. There are industries which involve danger to those employed, such as that of the miner, that of the sailor, that of the iron-worker; and it seems impossible for human society to continue without these pursuits, or to take from them the element of danger, so that altruistic persons might be free to allow others to engage in them. Certainly, if the highest morality is to do nothing and allow nothing to be done which may shorten human life or interfere with its comfort and happiness, the perfectly evolved social organism would have to make a fixed law that no man should be exposed to the danger of drowning, or of being killed or maimed in mines or burned in making steel. We have not yet reached the point of calling these occupations heroic; we reserve that praise for signal instances of courage when danger is far greater or the motive is nobler. But although Mr. Spencer does in one place admit that there will be room for heroism, although he might willingly give the name of hero to every sailor and miner and blast-furnaceman,—that will not help his theory. Society could not demand heroism. To demand it would be immoral. As every militant period, every war, is inconsistent with the happiness-evolution theory, so every dangerous occupation is a flat denial of it. The perfectly evolved society of Mr. Spencer would be an aggregate of people who never allowed each other to run the risk of going without a meal or catching cold or sleeping on anything but a down bed. So far as we can see, that is just a little beyond the possibilities of this world.

Now, to see the force of this, let it be remembered that under any hedonistic scheme the continuance of physical life is the first and most important object. Mr. Spencer speaks much of complete living, but in the background there is always the confession, which here we drag to the front, that the supremely important thing for a man is to live long.[1] Those conditions being secured under which a man shall have a long life, the next thing is to give him, if possible, a complete life. The best men have hitherto believed that complete life was the thing of greatest importance; not bare physical existence. They felt themselves bound to be true, to be brave, to be unselfish at all hazards. They would have considered it base to live if life meant falsehood, treachery, cowardice. Under the influence of this belief a strong, brave race was a possibility; but under Mr. Spencer's theory prolonging life is of so much importance that the social organism can promise to be nothing better than a nursery of valetudinarians. Complete living is paraded. We are assured that, since the social state gives space for and invites the pleasures of beneficence, men will seek them and complete life by their means. But if the great point is to keep death at bay, it follows that men will do such things, and such only, as conduce to long life. So the courage, the fidelity to truth, the heroic devotion to principle that have distinguished the best of men in the past will disappear. We shall have the complete living of the average sensuous man. Everthing will be discountenanced that might interfere with the comfort of people to whom longevity is the dearest of all desires, and that which promotes it the only virtue. Such is the moralisation we are really promised. Accept the social organism of Mr. Spencer and there is no escape from it.

[1] Data, p. 14.

But perhaps the distinguishing feature of the social organism is pointed to when it is said that the complete living of each must consist with and conduce to the complete living of all. This means that each individual forming an essential part of the body politic will have to be considered by the others, but will find his happiness in serving the general good. His individuality, in short, will exist and energise within limits determined by the aim and movements of the whole society; and gradually the dependence of each upon the whole and the completion of the happiness of each by right relations to the whole will be so understood that there will be no rebellion against the decisions and actions of the social organism. Thus we have, besides the affirmation that society forms an organism, the denial that any individual is a complete organism. While the free development of individual character, opinions, and will must succumb to the necessities or claims of the whole society, yet the unit in this way reaches his own perfect life: in no other way can he reach it.

No wonder Socialists have seized with avidity on such a comfortable doctrine; they would have been blind indeed if they had not seen how well it serves their ends and expresses their particularly limited view of human relations. The absorption of individual in communal life, the subjugation of personal aims and private interests to those of the body politic, is precisely that paradise of the average human animal which Socialism dreams of. No doubt it is a sad affliction to

Mr. Spencer to discover that his philosophy has been turned to so bad a use, and he may well attempt to clear himself. For he sees only too plainly that Socialism would mean for him and all who think for themselves abject slavery to the will of the majority, and that majority so practical that it would have no hesitation in harnessing Pegasus to a market cart. The average mind would settle the fate and the task of the genius. The protests of Mr. Spencer, his vehement protests against the coming slavery have had little effect—and why? Because he has practically given the game to his antagonists. All he can do now is to avert checkmate for a time.

But we can assure our author that, however much genius and talent might resent the rule of the materialistic crowd, they would yet endure it more patiently than conscience fired by the traditions of heroic valour and suffering for truth, conscience aware of its own high descent and scorning to be ruled by public vote. Let him comfort himself by remembering the Christians. The opposition to the threatened despotism of the average sensuous man is in firmer hands than his own. If we are to be mere parts of an organism, then we must bid adieu to our human prerogatives and powers, and that we will never do. Esau selling his birthright did at least get a dish to himself. We should have to barter all that makes life worth having for leave to dip a spoon in society's mess of pottage. The hard-won gains of human history will not be so lightly renounced.

But the whole theory of the social organism is ridiculous. Who ever heard of an organism consisting of an indefinite number of units every one of which has its own head and brains, its own independent will? Much as it is in favour with some people, it is really not worth consideration, and we may dismiss it as a mere parable not in any sense scientific. At the same time let us not fail to observe that if this notion of the social organism is necessary to Mr. Spencer's scheme of moralisation, then his whole theory splits here. And it is necessary; for without it the progress of altruistic pleasure-seeking cannot be assumed.

5. *Each Man a Species.*

We here come to a question of great importance in our discussion, and in others going on just now. Physiologically no doubt human beings constitute one species; our anatomists, microscopically examining every part of the body, have established that. But if like attention were paid to intellectual, moral, and emotional facts, would it not be clear that each individual of the human race is in truth a separate species— an example of variation establishing itself and continuing in a distinct line? Between man and man considered physically the differences are slight. Against the physical similarities, however, are to be set the psychological differences, and these are very great. It is time that this fact were recognised and the relations of human beings considered in the full light of it. There is much talk of altruism—perfectly sympathetic brotherhood to come by evolution. But what if evolution has for its task to deepen and emphasise the specific differences between man and man? It has made those differences so far; must it not go on increasing them?

Professor Haeckel, in his "History of Creation," has pointed out how greatly human individuals differ. "If," he says, "the children of a human family show, even at the beginning, certain individual inequalities which we may consider as the consequence of individual adaptation, they will appear still more different at a later period of life when each child has passed through different experiences and has adapted itself to different conditions. . . . Two brothers, of whom one is brought up as a workman and the other as a priest, develop quite differently in body as well as in mind."[1] Again he says :—" The divergences of the child-organism from the parental form are so striking that, as a rule, we may designate them as monstrosities."[2] Now, in Professor Haeckel's view, the elasticity of the species is great enough to cover all variations in the mental as well as the physical organisation of men; but against this we contend that the distinctions between one and another due to the vigour of the will, the acuteness of consciousness, and established functions are such that the term *species* which is used to indicate the resemblance of one beech-tree to another is utterly confusing and inappropriate when applied to human beings. It

[1] History of Creation, vol. i. p. 233.   [2] Ibid., p. 229.

affirms a precise agreement of part with part, function with function, process with process among the included organisms, an identity of vital development under equal conditions. Such agreement, however, does not exist between man and man except on the surface—in regard to those matters which do not enter into their peculiar and proper life. To class men in one species because of these outer similarities is to neglect radical distinctions which are of the utmost importance in social life, in ethics, and in religion. Between two men outwardly much alike, physically of the same species, and so far as their animal nature is concerned equally developed, there may be no similarity of intellectual purpose or moral temper. They differ as much, they are as far from understanding each other, as the ant from the bee or the ape from the fox. Professor Haeckel, we have seen, goes so far as to say that every child-organism appears as a monstrosity, unique in the race. He practically admits, therefore, the starting-point of a species in each case, and the progress of life establishes the species.

The activities of the human personality are such as to give each individual that separateness from others which is the proper mark of species. He is different in temperament, in habit, in mental bias, in moral quality. He is different by heredity, by education, by the development or the want of æsthetic sensibility, by association with others, by love and hatred, fear and hope. The higher you rise in the scale the less is a man guided by accepted formulæ, the more does he

THE LOWER BIOLOGY. 95

glory in striking out an independent path, if not in daily observance, yet decisively in that realm of thought and emotion where his real life springs up and becomes fruitful. A man is a man here, first and last. Is there any formula that will cover all the activities of the whole human race? Can there ever be such a formula? There can,—if individuality is to be suppressed, if genius is to be obliterated, if every human life is to be crushed into one mould; not otherwise. The resemblance is striking between Mr. Spencer, whose "Data of Ethics" assumes the possibility of such a formula, and the Pharisee of our Lord's time who, in this respect at least, anticipated evolutionary philosophy. To him it was a matter of conviction that one code of rules might be made to fit every man, whose perfection would consist in conforming to it. Mr. Spencer's expression, "a formula for complete life," is precisely such as an eminent Pharisee might have used, so marvellously does the cycle of human thought return on old notions. But in the exact degree of Mr. Spencer's resemblance to the Pharisee is the opposition between his rabbinism and the "law of life that is in Christ Jesus." Over against the Pharisee stood the Master, speaking the few deep words that went straight and with inspiring force to each human personality; and over against the scientific pharisaism of our day, with its gemara and phylacteries, there is still the living "Word of God," a liberating quickening power in each separate human spirit.

So the conservation of happinesses can never unite

men into a harmonious society, nor can any scheme of progress be founded on that principle. For just here —in respect of the happiness they desire and esteem —the specific differences of human beings are most marked. Mr. Spencer says, in his chapter on "Equilibration"[1]:—"Each advance in mental evolution is the establishment of some further internal action, . . . some additional connection of ideas or feelings answering to some before unknown or unantagonised connection of phenomena. We inferred that each such new function involving some new modification of structure implies an increase of heterogeneity, and that thus increase of heterogeneity must go on. . . . It can come to an end only as equilibration is completed." So he proceeds to consider the "fate towards which all things tend;"—exhaustion of the force which expends itself in adjusting man to society and society to man, that is, "omnipresent death." Well, it is by perpetual differentiation that man's life advances, "varied activities in achieving special ends marking his progress;" and of necessity the happiness which governs these activities must be more and more differentiated. In plain language, variation in happiness must keep pace with evolution; if the one is an affair of increasing heterogeneity, so must the other be. The well-being of the tribe governed all in the beginning, and the individual was merged in the tribe. From this early condition progress has been made on the line of liberating the individual and developing him up to the full

[1] First Principles, p. 513.

limit of his powers; and if happiness controls this progress there is with every generation an increasing departure from the original state in which happiness was, so to speak, communal. We are not all hunters and warriors now; and with our different kinds of pursuits and differently developed character we have widely different ideals of enjoyment. Yet the whole contention of Mr. Spencer implies that happiness is to be communal or whatever it was in the first ages. Individual life and liberty, developed at so much expense, are to be swallowed up, and all enjoyments and aspirations, however noble, are to be suppressed, for the sake of obtaining that egoistic satisfaction which the average sensuous man will allow.

Now, against this scheme or forecast stands the barrier of species, the truth that each individual is specifically different from all others; and the contention that it does so is thoroughly supported by the passage cited from the "First Principles." If by differentiation I become a complete, unique, effective person, then my happiness also must be personal, unique. Between the development of personality on the one hand and communal happiness on the other the choice must be made; they cannot go on together. By the theory of evolution, on which Mr. Spencer founds everything, varieties of happiness, like varieties of animal life, are species in the making, and progress means the development of innumerable species of human enjoyment. Only, therefore, if he is prepared to affirm that all the species of men and animals are gradually to return by degeneration through lower and lower forms to the original monad can he assert that happiness is to become less varied, to degenerate through lower and lower forms until it shall be entirely homogeneous—or anything like it.

Turning to practical life—do we not find all the facts to be on the side of the doctrine that there are specific differences between men and their happinesses and that these must increase? By what law, what necessity, am I bound to consider the gratification of a philosopher whose great object is to persuade me that Christ is superseded and that my faith in Him is a vain superstition? Minor admissions, even though I made them, would not content such an opponent. He demands success in proving God to be unknowable and happiness the one basis of moralisation. If I am altruistic towards him, it can only be in the way of accepting his theory and helping him to preach it. He enjoins me to be rational, and I admit the duty. But then, in helping the education of the race, I shall feel it necessary to show men that they must turn his philosophy out of doors; and how will his happiness be served in that case? Does Mr. Spencer ever try to make Christians happy, say Mr. Spurgeon, or Mr. Hugh Price Hughes, or the Bishop of Bedford? They are organic enough; they have great pleasure in their activities; they are engaged in altruistic work and find egoistic delight in it. Evolution has produced them, and they seem to fulfil all the terms of the Spencerian category. Why, then, does not Mr. Spencer become a member of

THE LOWER BIOLOGY.   99

the Tabernacle or help in a London "Mission"? Such other-regarding actions would "conduce to self-regarding gratifications by generating a genial environment." Then there are the Socialists, who detest what they are pleased to call "*bourgeois*" notions of comfort and respectability. It is not likely, we suppose, that Mr. Spencer will go far to meet their wishes; all which is very singular after one has read the "Data of Ethics."

Or let us take the case of an Ultramontane priest :— What would be our relation to him under the rule of mutual accommodation? Justice, to be treated simply as a fellow-man, would not content him. Tolerance he despises. He demands acceptance of his theory of religion, admission of his authority as a priest to direct, confess, absolve. It is idle to talk about making it possible for that man to "rear the due number of progeny" and live comfortably on the common level. To give him the power he desires would mean for Mr. Spencer abjuring the Synthetic Philosophy or going to the stake. There is no resource but to contest every claim made by the priest on behalf of himself and his Church, though he should be pained to the quick. In effect, therefore, we have not simply species but genera and generic differences among men. And if evolution perpetuates and increases those differences, as we must certainly expect it will, if conflicts and divisions continue to mark the energising of humanity, what evolutionary philosopher will dare to call this bad or immoral?

The business of evolution in the past has been, as we

have said, to liberate and develop the individual, to produce and foster innumerable species of men. All experiments in living, reformations, revolutions, progress in knowledge and art, attempts at political justice, have been doing this for us:—they have been making room for the individual and giving him the means of achieving more distinct and noble personal life. Mr. Ruskin's accusations against the methods of modern industry, that they cramp the mind of the workman, must not be forgotten. But there is compensation for the majority in opportunities for self-culture and in the wide diffusion of science and literature. When a certain task is done the artisan is free, and shows that he is free, to go where his own tastes may direct and do what his own desires may prompt. There has been less and less restraint on personal activity, provided only that certain rules necessary for the working of society were observed. Illustrations of this will suggest themselves to every reader, and it is needless to go into detail. The claims made by women in our century may be mentioned by way of example. Is Mr. Spencer's view of evolution the true one? If so, we have been priding ourselves on a *cultus* of the individual which is a harmful superstition and must go speedily to the limbo of vanities. One of our author's disciples, who is also a critic, has indeed assured us that so it is, and that the air must be purified by revolution. Without that, he says, the social organism can never be rightly organised. Revolution accomplished, all reduced to the same necessity of making things comfortable for each other and

THE LOWER BIOLOGY. 101

getting self-gratification by other-regarding actions, the reign of the average man would begin. The work of the great nations having gone by the board, life would become an affair of what may be generally liked,—as they say of fashions in clothes.

6. *Are we stronger as we are happier?*

Taking him all in all, Mr. Spencer must be held to maintain that vigour of life goes along with good actions—that is to say, joy-promoting actions. In the first place, he says so repeatedly, although the audacity of the statement frightens himself when he sees it written, and he has to glide at once into various qualifications. In the second place, he needs to maintain this, and to do so without any qualifications, for his whole scheme of a perfect human society depends upon it. Well, let us examine the " Data of Ethics " and see how the position is held.

We quote again the affirmations: " It is demonstrable that there exists a primordial connection between pleasure-giving acts and continuance or increase of life, and, by implication, between pain-giving acts and decrease or loss of life."[1] " Sentient existence can evolve only on condition that pleasure-giving acts are life-sustaining acts."[2] He pointedly repels the astonishment we are likely to feel at this " naked enunciation of an ultimate truth underlying all estimates of right and wrong," and is severe upon those who allow their minds to dwell

[1] Data, p. 82. [2] Ibid., p. 83.

upon the exceptions and not upon the rule. Again :—
"Every pleasure increases vitality; every pain decreases
vitality; every pleasure raises the tide of life; every
pain lowers the tide of life."[1] So life has been evolved
and maintained in the past; so human life must be
maintained and evolved till its perfect moralisation shall
be reached.

Having made these bold, universal affirmations, the
reasoner might be expected to go on with proof and
illustration. But, strange to say, he has to give his
attention for some time to "anomalies," "failures,"
"exceptions." He has to allow that there are mischievous pleasures and beneficent pains. It turns out
that in quite a number of cases the desire for happiness
betrays and misleads instead of guiding life towards the
highest efficiency and vigour. He partially examines a
very few of these cases because they really cannot be
ignored, and he would fain prove them to be merely incidental and temporary. Our conclusion from a wider
survey will be, that in human life the rule he affirms can
certainly be discovered, but only in the lowest ranges of
activity, and that Mr. Spencer's "biological" interpretations are altogether inadequate.

Our author himself admits that there are in human
development two great transitions in the course of
which individuals have to endure pain, have to be continually adjusting themselves with difficulty to fresh
conditions, and, in short, are often very miserable—for
the sake of evolution. These transitions are from the

[1] Data, p. 87.

THE LOWER BIOLOGY. 103

nomadic to the settled, and from the militant to the industrial way of life; and in both there has been a failure of guidance by pleasures and pains. There is, indeed, a general break down of the great principle; the wheels of evolution run backward for a time and a fresh start has to be made. Here is a fine confession, one involving much more than Mr. Spencer gives his readers to suppose. The examples chosen are treated in a very abstract way, and he is careful only to mention such as will fall in with his whole scheme. But if, instead of being general and vague, he had taken particular cases, he would have found himself at once in serious difficulty. The Hebrew people at the Exodus deliberately entered upon a course for which their previous history had not prepared them, sacrificing almost their whole hoard of satisfactions for the sake of an idea. In the wilderness as a nomadic, militant race they had all the difficulties of a new beginning, and the generation which left Egypt and had the brunt of the change to bear never enjoyed its advantages. We call the Exodus a striking evolutionary departure. But there is no explanation of it in the law of happiness culture. Under that law they should have adapted themselves to Egyptian rule and modified those national traits which interfered with their comfort. Clearly their life in the wilderness was made possible, not by what they had enjoyed in Egypt, but by what they had suffered; and the gratifications of Egypt, so far as they were remembered, did not help the people in the least, but, on the contrary, made them uncertain and discontented. In this familiar bit of history we have a type of movements continually taking place, movements governed by some idea, some high evolutionary strain not springing from physical happiness nor aiming at it. The history of every European nation affords examples of change nothing less than catastrophic if Mr. Spencer's theory be true, and yet in no sense compulsory. The Scottish Covenanters, to whom it was utter misery to fight, laid 'aside their implements of husbandry and took the field against a government they would have been glad to obey if an idea had not filled their minds. Evolution, to these people, meant leaving comfortable homes and a peaceful, orderly way of life; it drove them, without the least military training, to risk a desperate conflict in which many of them were sure to fall. They stand now as types of folly to some persons, and the reason, we suppose, is the spread of Mr. Spencer's opinions. Italy, again, should have accommodated herself to the Pope, Bomba, and the Austrians, turned a deaf ear to Garibaldi, and stolidly given her mind to crops and trade. Her choice time after time was for—catastrophe.

If happiness promoted vitality, if it raised the tide of life, as it is said to do, the people who enjoyed most should certainly have been the most energetic people, always in the van the world over. The changes that took place ought always to have been such as they shaped and determined. A nation poor, uncivilised, inhabiting a sterile country, should never have had success against one more prosperous and comfortable.

The whole course of things ought to be for the extinction of unhappy communities. But has it been so? Does not the world owe most to small, hardy independent nationalities, poor in everything but spirit? And have we not heard about the decay of empires through luxury and the cultivation of happiness? Clearly, when evolution settles a race of men into habits of enjoyment it is not preparing them for the time of trial which is certain to follow. On the other hand, those who have received few of the favours of evolution, never rising to that fine vitality which pleasure is said to create, those inured to privation and toil, the serfs of nature, are ready for the hour of change.

Now, of course, it will be maintained, in opposition to the argument here suggested, that people often prefer their own ideas to any imposed on them from outside; that it is their happiness to take their own way. Oh yes, it will be said of the Covenanters,—a dour, egotistic, factious crew, they cared for nothing except the maintenance of that bigotry which they were pleased to call religion. It was their happiness to be irreconcilable fanatics and to give wiser men no peace. And in like manner, it will be said, the Jews in the time of the Maccabees preferred to fight for the temple and the laws, and found their pleasure so rather than in submitting to the Syrians and having a fairly comfortable life. And that is an argument which gets rid of all difficulty so far. But then if we are to reckon guidance by happiness in that way there is nothing left to discuss. Men submit to be slaves, and that is happiness; they rush on spears, and that also is happiness. What is happiness, and what is evolution? The new utilitarianism is always to play a winning game, is it? Heads I win; tails you lose!

7. *Thou shalt procrastinate!*

Here, however, we have to face yet another theory, one based on "the relative authority of motives."[1] In the whole ascent of life from the lowest creatures up to the highest man, we are told, immediate sensations have been more and more subjected to the ideas of future sensations; there has been an overruling of the immediate by the representative. Animals began by snatching at the nearest satisfactions and avoiding the nearest pains, men go on to consider far-away possibilities of pleasure or deliverance from pain and adapt their actions with greater cunning and cleverness to secure those remote advantages. And the ideal feelings thus kindled in their minds somehow have authority, order them about in fact, take control of their lives. They are a bridge by which nations or individuals cross easily and safely those difficult passages in their history when enjoyments have to be renounced and new habits formed. Actual pleasures not being available, in order to sustain their vitality they imagine pleasures, or rather imaginary pleasures occupy their minds. It is as when a hungry man dreameth, and behold he eateth. Only the dream is a day-dream, and masters him. If he sought the pleasures now for

[1] Data, p. 108.

which he has been fitted by his history he would be altogether at fault. But he does not; being an evolved man, he cannot. He is guided by imaginations. "With approach to the highest types present ends become increasingly subordinate to those future ends which the ideal motives have for their objects."[1] In truth, if the highest type of man had not to think of the needs of his body he would have his gaze always fixed upon the "dim and distant future," held in rapt anticipation of joys unattainable in the present. Yet this is the man who can never repeat an action or contract a habit or retrace a line of thought unless it brings at once relief from pain or increase of pleasure. These are the doings of mind, "combinations of stimuli, somewhat variable in their modes of union, leading to complex notions similarly variable in their adjustments," the weighing of possibilities, the balancing of feelings.

Still the principle is sound. In fact, we would say that, carried far enough, it is exceedingly like the Christian principle of looking not at things seen and temporal, but at things unseen and eternal, the principle of faith in things not seen as yet and in the Divine promises by which they are presented to the view. And Christianity, erecting a noble goal, has this recommendation, that it holds admirably the balance between the near and the remote, prescribes clear and intelligible laws by which the degree of attention to near and distant objects of desire is to be governed. But at this point how fares evolution in its attempt

[1] Data, p. 109.

to guide men? By its apostle's own confession, it is reduced to a series of miserable ifs and mays. "Grant that, working his brain unceasingly from dawn till dark, the man in pecuniary difficulties must disregard rebellious bodily sensations in obedience to the conscientious desire to liquidate the claims on him; yet he *may* carry this subjection of simple feelings to complex feelings to the extent of shattering his health, and failing in that end which, with less of this subjection, he *might* have achieved."[1] And that is serious, for if conscientiousness were "fatal" it would be, of all immoral guiding principles, the most immoral. Death ends all happiness. Nor is it to be forgotten that the nation or man enduring hardship in some crisis, sacrificing pleasure for conscience' sake, or bravely contending against adverse circumstances, in privation and, so far as this world is concerned, without hope, must of necessity be wrong. The icy formula by which the evolutionary moralist damns every valiant struggler is this:—"Pain is the correlative of some species of wrong—some kind of divergence from that course of action which perfectly fulfils all requirements."[2]

But the leading principle of the "Data of Ethics" is involved here, and it cannot be accommodated so easily as Mr. Spencer would have us believe to the control of ideal and distant motives. Assure men that evolution is aiming at happiness and they will soon conclude that, since "life is good or bad according as it does or does not bring a surplus of agreeable feeling,"[3] the

[1] Data, p. 111.   [2] Ibid., p. 260.   [3] Ibid., p. 27.

enjoyment which can be had at once without trouble is to be preferred to the enjoyment which can only be had at some indefinitely remote period after a great deal of trouble. If, with this pleasure theory to guide him, any one throws over altruism as too troublesome, chooses a kind of life which implies the least possible risk along with the greatest comfort, he can defy our philosopher to prove him in the wrong. The miser is a product of evolution. He may be abnormal, but he is there, and within the limits of human activity he seeks and finds his "pleasure." But, setting aside cases which may be described as abnormal, is the evolutionist entitled to condemn those who spend their time in a round of dainty frivolity and highly organised enjoyment? From Mr. Spencer's point of view a large quantity of second-rate pleasure must needs be more useful than a small quantity which is of a finer kind, even if it has the recommendation of being connected with representative and re-representative feelings. The prudent rake, in fact, who is careful not to injure his health, is obeying the law of happiness better than the enthusiastic philanthropist who dies early. Pleasure as a guide is most uncertain, and, failing a higher law, neither altruistic safeguards on the one hand nor egoistic on the other can be relied on to keep life in the way of greatest effectiveness and elaborated enjoyment. In brief, the eleventh commandment, according to Mr. Spencer, is, Thou shalt enjoy putting off thy pleasure:—but there is no thunder.

8. *How can an evolutionist predict?*

What is the chief factor in human evolution? Is it experience or aspiration, the conservation of chance gains or the desire for unrealised conditions?

Certainly a complex state of society, such as that of any European country at the present time, does suggest to some men remote aims, and urges all who are prudent to provide against future needs of themselves and families. The efforts of those who are caught in the attraction of luxury or power take one direction, the efforts of those who are fascinated by the hope of artistic or literary fame take quite another line; and those who would avoid the misery of dependence must often renounce every other desire in order to acquire a little money. But these activities, induced by the conditions of society, do not necessarily improve the existing conditions; their sole object and result may be to suit the individual to the actual state of things. Even although there is a reaching into the future, that does not imply a wish or purpose to make life happier for other people. Evolution is the ruler, not the ruled; it prophesies nothing; it says: Man, adapt yourself to what is; and, apart from Christianity, only a few persons will be found troubling themselves with schemes for the future, schemes just as likely to be mischievous as useful.

For with the mass of men practical necessity is the great thing. They have always the business of the day

THE LOWER BIOLOGY.

to pursue, some urgent personal aim. And since evolution depends on the habits and experiments of the mass of men, not on the notions of a few philosophers, it is utterly impossible to count on beneficent aspiration as a factor of any weight. We speak here in terms of that philosophy which makes all past progress the result of experience; and the future progress conformable to such a view of the past and such a philosophy can only be that which is due to the accumulation of unforeseen or chance gains. It is utterly impossible to find in mechanical evolution the ground of any hope worth indulging for an hour. Mr. Spencer appears to think that evolution somehow produces infallible aspirations, that, blindly aware of coming good, she whispers to her children the secret of happiness indefinitely remote and urges them on the way that will at length bring mankind to a goal of complete enjoyment. His own system is an interpretation of such a whisper. But he only dreams. On the basis of materialism he might just as well argue that in a few generations men will be weary of life before they are thirty, and the great art will be that of euthanasia. We have already quoted some of Mr. Spencer's predictions, and we might quote many more; there are pages of them. He tells us that certain things must happen, and certain others will. "Every one," we heard, "who leaves behind primitive dogmas and primitive ways of looking at things, . . . who has acquired those habits of thought which science generates, . . . will infer that the type of nature to which the highest social life affords a sphere such that every faculty has its due amount, and no more than the due amount, of function and accompanying gratification, is the type of nature towards which progress cannot cease till it is reached."[1] "Such a man," we are assured, "will find it impossible to believe that the processes which have heretofore moulded all beings"—to the social conditions Mr. Spencer declares good—"will not hereafter continue so moulding them." And so we have not simply prophecy, but the utmost dogmatism of prophecy. Irrationality, wrongness, absurdity, are charged against people who do not see as he sees or dream as he dreams; nor is it the least curious element in his dogmatism that he pours contempt on a large·class of thinkers whose aspirations and efforts have at least the authority of long trial and wide acceptance.

There is amongst us a foresight of remote good; there is a wise, generous ideal of complete life for which many are toiling and denying themselves, sacrificing much present enjoyment for the advantage of the whole race; multitudes of men and women are looking and labouring for the "remoulding of human nature."[2] On what principle is the Christian scheme of ethics and aspiration to be set aside as vain and foolish? Christianity certainly keeps a balance between desire for present enjoyment and pursuit of great far-off ends; and if Christianity dogmatises, so does the "Data of Ethics." Why are we bound to believe that Christian supernaturalism must vanish, and that the supernaturalism of Mr. Spencer must prevail?

[1] Data, p. 186.   [2] Ibid., p. 183.

THE LOWER BIOLOGY.

In the earlier stages of his philosophy our author had much to say about religion. Did he introduce his equivocal and superstitious worship of the unexhausted possibilities of force—the Unknowable of his system—as a means of restraining the too eager desires of men and refining their earthliness when Christianity shall be forgotten? He might well attempt something of the kind, for what do we see already in quarters where that religion is in temporary discredit? Why, the balance is lost; there is a growing discontent, expressed here in Socialism, there in a feverish clutching at enjoyment. Among those whose pleasures are few, who have to work hard and live poorly, impatience is increasing; they believe that they have not their share of the world's good, and they want to have it. The same craving for immediate happiness governs many who have culture, intelligence, all the resources of art and literature. So far from being ruled by the Spencerian philosophy, which they profess to admire, people are refusing to defer their own pleasures a single day, are throwing off all considerations of far-away gain, either their own moral strength or the good of the race. Art, which ministers so largely to this class, is ceasing to be ideal; literature, which aims at pleasing them, is becoming "naturalistic," shameless. From sensuous experiments men pass to sensual; the distant is renounced for the near, the beautiful for the intense, the noble for the novel and risky. If evolution is doing anything in this age, apart from Christianity, it is reducing all estimations to a material standard, the test of immediate results. The artist, the politician, the poet, are looking for the applause of society, for quick returns of fame, opportunity, and wealth, and the whirl of sordid effort and sensuous craving goes faster every day. Yet out of this we are bidden expect an evolution of placid beneficence and serene co-operation. Let those hope who do not study the times, who do not give attention to facts—or, who can trust in a Living God.

9. *The real law of pleasure distribution.*

In opposition to the whole contention of Mr. Spencer, this is clear on a survey of life, that happiness does not of necessity either guide or follow "Evolution," that it is attached neither to morality nor immorality, neither to progress nor retrogression, but is distributed impartially, so to speak, like air and sunshine, to be used or abused by men as they themselves may determine. It is simply a condition of sentient life. In like manner pain is distributed not as the accompaniment of action which is bad or wrong, but as necessary in the relation of mind to body and external nature, with the effect of giving depth of feeling, emphasis, and power to life in its higher ranges.

Taking the distribution of pleasure, observe first what goes on in a London music-hall where a crowd is gathered seeking compensation for the hard work of the day. The domestic sentimental song may be applauded, but so is the vile rubbish that seems alto-

THE LOWER BIOLOGY.

gether beneath the human level, neither rhyme nor music deserving of the name. The worse the ditty, in many instances, the greater the pleasure; the lower the buffoon can descend, if he only manages to hit the fancy of the multitude and gratify the craving for mere dissipation, the more complete his success. Nor is it any better at a fashionable theatre, where an actress, of no small ability in a certain line, devotes herself body and mind to the impersonation of a character revoltingly immoral and uses all the arts at her command to assist in what is nothing but a prostitution of herself. To such an exhibition the West End sends nightly a throng of titled and wealthy people, parents, sons, and daughters; and half the conversation of the *beau monde* is of that admired actress and the depraving incidents of the play. The same people will also attend an oratorio, criticise the singers just as they criticised the actress and enjoy the "performance" as such. To a musical enthusiast equal pleasure is probably given by the play and the oratorio. Here pleasure is obviously quite apart from morality; to what evolution it points we leave Mr. Spencer to say. He would have us believe[1] that the cases in which pleasures and pains, sensational and emotional, serve as incentives to proper acts and deterrents from improper acts are "many and conspicuous," and that it is only in unessential matters that pleasures mislead. All we can say, with the pleasures of fashionable and unfashionable society in view, is that his notions of essential and non-essential

[1] Data, p. 84.

matters and of well-working and ill-working must be very singular for a moralist.

Again, consider present-day literature and the evidence offered by a novel of the "realist" school. First, we shall say, the writer had pleasure in producing it, pleasure exactly proportioned to the boldness with which he defied conventional ideas of morality in the scenes he described and the relations of his characters. It continues to give him pleasure in the degree of its popularity and the money return it brings. Then it gives pleasure to many readers; but of what kind? To those who read it for the story, as we say, it yields the joy of excitement. To others who know more of vice and vicious ways it affords keener delight. It gives them new sensations in a field which had seemed exhausted. Again, society is tickled with something fresh, and drawing-room conversation is furnished with matter in the contrasts that can be drawn and the opinions which can be expressed. The languor of social circles is relieved; the most vacuous have something to say about the universal topic. In short, activity and happiness are distinctly increased over a wide area. Of course there are some people who read to their misery, but their misery is relieved by the stimulus of virtuous indignation; and we may suppose the latter emotion to counteract those of disgust and loathing so far that the fleshly novel produces happiness all round. There is no doubt, at all events, that from first to last it is associated with a quantity of stimulating emotion. The same remarks will apply to certain pictures. In

THE LOWER BIOLOGY. 117

connection with vile novels circulated and vile dramas produced there must be a very great amount of enjoyment which does not excite to "proper acts." Right feeling may be sometimes stirred; but when there is increase of moral vigour there will be least pleasure, a mere surplus with difficulty asserted over a strong feeling of disgust. So, if the world-scheme is for pleasure the planning and publication of the vile story, giving intensity of feeling of a pleasurable kind, have the same justification as the existence of the human race itself. But on this basis what shall we say of such a man as General Gordon? He left his friends, risked his health, endured privations, and finally met a violent death in Central Africa. Judged by the happiness that resulted to himself and those associated with him, he was an ignominious blunderer as compared with the novelist.

Two main elements of happiness among savages and civilised people alike, at the West End as well as the East, are novelty and vivacity. While the chief business of life goes on by accommodations to the inevitable, in a sober, often a tragic way, people turn aside as often as they can to seek the novel and vivacious. But everywhere novelty and vivacity, in which happiness is sought, are just as likely to hinder as to help true progress. They do not make for general considerateness, tenderness, and equality of treatment. In no sense do they make for ideal purity either in art or conduct. And does any one suppose that the search for what is new and sparkling will make human life dignified or robust? Strength is not gained along that line, and the advancing societies are not those devoted to pleasure-seeking. It is a commonplace of modern writing this; and yet, spite of it, Mr. Spencer seems to imagine that by means of something not usually thought of as happiness at all the deliberate pursuit of happiness will be corrected in the case of those to whom enjoyment is all. People seek the novel and vivacious and are happy, —often improperly so. They also know the advantage of conciliating and helping each other; but this is rather a dull and ordinary business on the whole and may even be very disappointing. Now, Mr. Spencer's only hope for mankind is that keener satisfaction will be found in paying the sanitary inspector than in going to a concert at the Albert Hall, in reading a dull treatise on morality for the sake of gratifying the author than in reading a lively novel to please one's self. As people make this kind of choice easily they are becoming moralised; when they do so by sheer habit, instinctively, they will be in heaven, the only heaven they can attain. Such a condition of general comfort and accommodation will arrive, says Mr. Spencer, must arrive some time, because the whole course of evolution travels to that point. There will be one moment at least in the long history of humanity

> "When man to man the warld o'er
> Shall brithers be for a' that."

But how does he say it is to come? Have we been supposing it necessary to row hard and spread our sails to the heavenly breezes that we might make way slowly against a stream? That is altogether a delusion. We have but to commit ourselves cheerfully to the current, find our joy in its onward rush, and in good time the calm ocean shall be reached—by the stream. Concerning the individual there is no prophecy.

Here is a serious consideration. May we go on getting happiness without becoming more organic? May we go on getting happiness all our lifetime without aiding the evolution of the race? To both these questions Mr. Spencer should be able to return an unqualified *No*. Evolution has set us where we are. Evolution has made us what we are, body and mind. Such is the hypothesis. The great law is said to be that to enjoy and to go on becoming more capable of enjoyment will lead us in a way beneficial to ourselves and the race. Now, suppose this to be true. Can I, then, defy evolution? Can I seek and obtain happiness all my life which shall have no bearing on my own greater effectiveness as a social unit, nor on the moralisation of others? Can every one do so? Where, then, is the exception and where is the law? Evolution, *c'est moi*. If I have pluck enough or am lazy enough, *c'est moi*. There stands the obstinate fact which all the laboured arguments of the "Data of Ethics" attempt in vain to conceal. Not infrequently in the course of Mr. Spencer's divagations we are visited with the suspicion that he believes himself able to influence the destinies of the race; that he would fain say: Evolution, *c'est* MOI.

10.—*Has evolution been a mistake?*

Before advancing further we have here a question to consider, a strange and significant question, which our author himself calls ultimate, and it is this:—Has evolution been a mistake?[1] Considering the basis of judgment he lays down in his definition of good and bad conduct, it is little wonder that the inquiry occurs; yet he nowhere answers it distinctly. He declares that he has "uttered no judgment concerning the issue,"[2] and that, for the purpose of the argument, "no such judgment is called for." "By the general argument," he says, "I have tacitly committed myself to the optimistic view;" and the "tacit optimism" which pervades the "Data of Ethics" has, he thinks, "a wider basis" than some of his critics recognise. He allows that on the answer to the question whether life is worth living "depends entirely every decision concerning the goodness or badness of conduct." . . . "If it is held that there had better not have been animate existence at all," then in effect there can be no morals. But in answer to Mr. Sidgwick, who insists that he is "not establishing morality on a scientific basis," he simply repeats that if life is worth living actions which maintain it are good, and, whether life is worth living or not, it is good to be as happy as we can. All through the book he affirms in varied phrases that "evolution has been and is still working towards the highest life;"

[1] Data, p. 26.   [2] Ibid., pp. 306, 307.

but if put to the wall he would be prepared to say :—I do not declare that the highest life and its happiness are worth having, I tacitly assume it; if you think otherwise you are welcome to your opinion. My concern is to argue skilfully on the basis of a great peradventure, and to seek anything in my pages beyond such an argument is absurd. Now, for our part, we have to go much deeper than this; we cannot ignore the question what evolution is doing for her children. For, if the measure of happiness achieved and progress towards perfect happiness are the sole tests of evolution, it would certainly appear to be a frightful mistake.

Far back in the evolutionary past, when animals were simpler, had fewer enemies and less difficulty in satisfying wants, happiness must have been great in proportion to the capacity for it. If there had been only a single race of animals incapable of preying on each other, though they were of a low type, happiness would have been diffused as it can never be under the law that produces so many kinds and types. Not only is there hostility among them, but there is also increased complexity, which means greater difficulty in satisfying needs; the perils of derangement, too, are multiplied, and the pains of injury and disappointment. Contrast the sloth or the serpent with man and the existence of the lower animal, taken year by year, is immensely superior in its freedom from pain and average of contentment. The life of an anaconda in a tropical swamp must be one of almost complete "happiness." Intellectual development brings with it greater consciousness of danger and innumerable desires which it is difficult or impossible to satisfy. Social life has its gratifications, but it has also anxiety, suspense, regret, impatience, defeat. In order to justify evolution Mr. Spencer would need to prove that civilisation is immediately for happiness, that every change has increased the sum of satisfactions. Take the changes which occurred during the extension of the Roman empire. No doubt they gave pleasure to some, and certain advantages to a very great number. But where is the evidence of that distinct gain of happiness to the generation concerned which would alone have justified the warfare and sufferings of any period? Even if the balance dipped on the right side, would not the evolution that crushed so many individuals still need defence? By Mr. Spencer's own admission the militant life is one of pain and privation; and the question is, not how evolution is to get rid of war and its accompanying evils, but how it ever allowed them. Of course there was the struggle for existence, but an evolution that is for happiness should have steadily prevented that from being sanguinary; it should have wrought by easier methods.

Coming nearer our own time, was the fifth century happier than the first? Is the nineteenth happier than the fourteenth? While the strain of life becomes continually greater, the minds of men more restless, the problems of being more pressing and involved, can it be said that evolution is justified in the increasing happiness of our age, allowing even, for the sake of argument, that all happiness is of a good kind?

"Humanity to-day," as Bishop Carpenter well says, "looks back upon the brightness of visions and hopes which it believes to have passed away. The sweet vision of its youth, when it looked into the eyes of heavenly wisdom and believed, is gone; the political hopes which more than a generation ago rose so high, when the dream of plenty and peace belonged to Europe, and when all things in political and social affairs seemed possible to the new-found vigour of emancipated communities, are gone; the door of the City of Flowers is closed upon society; distress, depression, doubt, is the portion of the age, exiled from its hope and its dream. Society, like the poet, has tried to climb the hill where perpetual sunlight falls, but the triple foes of luxury, ambition, and greed have proved too strong for its aspirations and endeavours. The path of bitter experience and of discomfited pride must be trodden."[1] Progress, then, has not led to happiness. We, testing evolution where alone we can test it, in our own state to-day, must needs affirm that there is a terrible mistake somewhere if happiness be the aim.

Or again, take the finest and most cultured specimens of humanity in contrast with the ruder and less developed. Has progress in happiness gone along with the intellectual and æsthetic advance? He would be a bold man who should say that talent, culture and genius blossom surely into enjoyment, serenity and hopefulness, or that such an issue is more common now than it was two thousand years ago. Yet if life advances

[1] *Contemporary Review*, December 1886, p. 368.

in the way supposed the man of science, of cultivated intelligence and artistic education should have higher vitality, greater buoyancy and delight in life than the artisan or the backwoodsman. It should not be possible to doubt for a moment whether of these is the happier man. No longer should the ploughboy or the milkmaid be the type of cheerful content; we ought to be far past the superstition which attributes to them the light and gladsome heart. When Wordsworth says—

> "Shades of the prison-house begin to close
>   Upon the growing boy,
> But he beholds the light and whence it flows,—
>   He sees it in his joy;
> At length the man perceives it die away
> And fade into the light of common day:"—

the mirth and sportiveness of every philosopher should testify against the ignorance of the poet. But how is it that as yet we see nothing of the new type even in embryo? One or two, indeed, have laboured to sustain the *rôle*, but they can hardly be said to have equalled the unlettered martyrs of early Christianity. And, to make a long story short, the students of evolution, who have left behind them many errors which entangled their predecessors in philosophy, should be far stronger and happier than was Socrates or Epicurus. To find a modern evolutionist oppressed with anxiety, writing gloomy political articles, not cheerful either about his country or about the world, doubtful even as to the prospects of his own philosophy, is to discover at least

THE LOWER BIOLOGY. 125

one notable piece of evidence that evolution is somehow missing the mark. But the search for the happiest people is no business of ours. It may be left to those who think enjoyment the matter of greatest importance; and they will have to pursue their inquiries in regions where the philosophers are little known and the contending schools of art have no partisans.

11. *Is Mr. Spencer a moralist?*

Not for a moment can it be maintained that natural evolution is making it more possible to live easily, comfortably, nor that greater complexity of life can ever mean greater joy all round. The immense amount of trouble which is necessary to keep the social machine in working order, the innumerable accidents to which, in spite of all care, it is subject, every one of them involving misery, or at least laborious counteraction, demonstrate the absurd futility of the Spencerian prediction. Nature and evolution are not kindly in the material sense, and there is no sign that they ever will be. The few evidences to be found, apart from Christianity, that forces are at work for the production of universal good-nature are utterly insufficient for the basis of a hope; they are, as we have shown, heavily counterbalanced. And suppose men did their best for each other in the way of mutual compromises, they could not touch the working of those stern and awful powers which at every turn necessitate patience, endurance, valour in the face of death. Nothing can alter or conceal the fact that human life here is a tragedy. The course of activity for multitudes is determined not by their present desire but by inexorable laws from which they cannot escape. They are in a current strong, resistless, bearing them not towards a sunny shore but towards the engulfing ocean. Much of their energy is absorbed in keeping themselves afloat; temporary relief from the struggle may be obtained by laying hold of a plank that is swept within reach, but it is soon water-logged or borne away by a swirl of the tide. Mr. Spencer pictures what men might do if they were their own masters. But the millions are not. The question of attaining happiness of the kind they most desire either immediately or at some future time has nothing to do with three-fourths of their activities. Without any reference to their pleasure they have to be early at work summer and winter under the pressure of what often appears a dire necessity. The wheels keep moving; their labour may produce some honest fabric or some miserable shoddy stuff, but whatever is the result they must toil on till they are tired. In the midst of the press and whirl, which show no sign of abating, evolution proceeds. The whirl is itself evolution. To expect it to slacken is as reasonable as to expect that the earth will cease revolving about the sun. The hope of an equilibrium is at best the hope of a brief and far-off moment in the history of the race. To help mankind towards such a moment of balanced happiness before descending the final slope,—can this offer any inducement to or exert any pull upon the individual whose own career has to be accomplished, whose own share has to be secured, speedily or never? As a moralist Mr. Spencer is bound to urge men up the slope towards purer, juster life, call it altruistic or what you will. As an evolutionist, with his eye clear to see the truth, he might have traced an urgency of this kind blending with nature, operating through all human experience, expressing itself in every wise law and ordinance of man. But as a preacher of happiness, what he does is to show men a downward course and bid them follow it with blind confidence. If he is rightly representing evolution we are not in a period of advance, but already in a period of decline. Our development must have passed its crest, and before us lies the facile descent of Avernus. To speak of the pull of happiness making men better is simply foolish talk. That can only lead them to evade trouble as far as possible at every step, to make all kinds of judicious pretences, to help themselves to everything they fancy and congratulate themselves that going downhill is easy work.

II.

THE REIGN OF HABIT.

Having so far considered Mr. Spencer's answer to the question how the golden age is to be reached, we will now examine his treatment of duty. In effect he says, "The equilibrium of happiness will assuredly come; things are as they are, and cannot fail to go in the line I indicate." But he also speaks of right and wrong; he has a code of ethics. It would appear that human choice has much to do with the millennium, which therefore will arrive only if we seek it and labour to establish it. And, for his own part, the moralist has a strong sense of obligation in connection with the business. He assumes the prophetic strain—the burden of the valley of vision.

Now, it might seem that if evolution is effecting the result we need not trouble ourselves in the least; a prophet would appear superfluous. Our author writes: —"I am the more anxious to indicate in outline, if I cannot complete this final work,"—my gospel, in fact, —"because the establishment of rules of right conduct on a scientific basis is a pressing need."[1] But why should an evolutionist be anxious about anything? Does he not deny the virtue of his own principle, which is necessitarian? When he speaks of *rules of right conduct*, the *controls of morality*, and so forth, is he not troubling us needlessly about a matter which the Power we can never know has in hand? We are assured that causal evolution is the infallible law of all change. If it be so, the interference of men by means of their theories is mere foolishness; to frame moral rules and devise precautions is only to complicate matters, as, indeed, we shall find our author allowing by-and-by. Suppose the moralist cunningly anticipates how

[1] Data, Preface, p. viii.

things are to go and gets a few to accept his previsions, may that not be to give them undue length of life and more than their proper share of pleasure? Here is a nervous, dyspeptic person, not fitted by constitution to form a strong link in the evolutionary chain. Mr. Spencer, we shall say, puts him in possession of an ethical secret by which he may protract his life, render himself agreeable by his judicious altruism and rear a family pedantically and nervously altruistic like himself. But is not this to prevent the comfort, the free development, perhaps the life of more eupeptic, more bold and vivacious persons of greater value to the race?

Whatever morality there is among the animals that dwell together in an island or among the fishes of the sea, it is spontaneous. They do not keep philosophers to draw up moral codes for their guidance in living according to nature. If they did, their limited views would certainly result in some very strange and perplexing experiments; the difficulties of our biologists would be multiplied a hundredfold. But we men are not all highly intelligent, and even our philosophers may entirely misread the facts of nature; trying to help evolution they may only block its way. And since among the ruminants and the fishes the law of evolution has, according to Mr. Spencer, done admirably without the aid of bovine or piscine data of ethics, ought not he as an evolutionist to let nature alone?

Nevertheless, in some strange doubt of the world-process, he is concerned and "anxious" to establish

I

the rules of right conduct "on a scientific basis;" to do so is a "pressing need,"—"the secularisation of morals is becoming imperative." "Few things," he says, "more disastrous can happen than the decay and death of a regulative system before another and fitter has grown up to replace it. . . . And as the change which promises or threatens to bring about this state is rapidly progressing, those who believe that the vacuum can be filled and that it must be filled are called on to do something in pursuance of their belief."[1] In short, evolution is in a difficulty. All-powerful as it is, universal as it is, there will be a "vacuum" unless some priest of its mysteries comes forward to reveal and recommend its laws. How very strange! A vacuum looks like the cessation of evolution, does it not? Or is Mr. Spencer, as the prophet of the age, a necessity supplied in the nick of time to prevent the collapse of everything?

One would have thought that when the code of supernatural ethics had disappeared, as a useless function dropped by advancing humanity, it would be more than absurd to produce another system to interfere yet again with the free play and energy of life. An evolutionist doing something in pursuance of a belief, and such a belief, affords a choice example of superstition, of sheer wrong-headedness that cannot be matched elsewhere and will some day be the cause of much conjecture, not to say amusement in scientific circles. Every rigorous thinker must here agree with a remark of Mr.

[1] Data, Preface, p. viii.

Green that when the speculative part of ethics has been reduced to a natural science the practical or preceptive part has been abolished altogether.[1] How can you call upon a being who is the product of physical necessity to shape the course of that necessity, to give form and direction to the energies by which his own little life is enveloped and constantly shaped? Mechanical evolution may be regarded either as the sum of absolutely necessary sequences or as a mere flux of change, the history of variations of which we can only say that they have been as they have been. Whichever way we look at it, precepts are useless and prophecy absurd. For, whether a dominating necessity in the evolution is or is not asserted, everything and every life must be allowed to be equally evolved; whatever is has the same right to be. It is useless to talk of a vacuum here and a need there. Anything evolution drops is done with; anything it provides is fit and right. To affirm that any process will be perilous is beside the mark; it betrays ignorance of the whole scheme. Evolution, if it overwhelmed the whole human race in some vast catastrophe or obliterated the cosmos known to us, would be justified. Mechanical processes, which are all in all according to Mr. Spencer's theory, would be serenely continued as if nothing had happened. If a thing is not, just now, it is because there is no present need for it; and if a thing I might do is not done, there is no need for it, my inertness being part of evolution. If one asserts that there is a vacuum

[1] Prolegomena to Ethics, p. 9.

and is anxious to fill it up, no doubt his anxiety is a necessity—to him. But if another says that there is no vacuum, no reason for anxiety, no occasion to exert himself, he is equally justified, his persuasion and indifference being as necessary as the anxiety of the other. Let men do nothing; let them lie in their beds from this hour and evolution will work on all the same. Let them use all the endeavours they can to keep human progress going in a certain line and evolution will laugh at their attempts and take her own way. For their "moralisation" and "equilibration" she cares no more than for the proper ebb and flow of the tides.

Such are incontestable deductions from the physical theory to which Mr. Spencer is committed. And when he hinges anything on human choice, forecasting what should be and appealing to men to aid in fulfilling his predictions, he is answered by every person who may say, "I care nothing for your forecast." An evolutionist acts absurdly in making human will a power apart from evolution or venturing on advice which any other person's experience has not forestalled, or may not sanction. The proper thing is to allow the nature and experience of each individual, who as a living being has his part in the scheme of things, to guide him freely, and to make no attempt whatever to prejudice him. Then out of the existing state of society, which is naturally perfect because it is, will grow another state equally necessary and perfect. But what that shall be the nature-evolutionist has nothing to do with, and cannot foretell any more than if he had lived in the carboniferous era he could have foretold the state of matters in the chalk period or justifiably tried to shape evolution towards it. His own belief is only an opinion, and his ignorance being well known to himself, he should be always aware that it is a thousand to one he will prove quite wrong.

Let us, however, admit the incomprehensible necessity of looking after evolution and coaxing her products to do their duty in the station of life to which it has pleased her to call them. So we can go on to consider the ethical scheme whereby the world is to reach a great and happy consummation. And there is offered to us first an account of the evolution of morality; second, a theory of moralisation apart from the sense of duty.

1. *Interpreting the more developed by the less developed.*

In the Spencerian sense conduct is simply action from a motive; it is defined as " acts adjusted to ends; " and in order to understand human conduct we are invited to study it as a part of that large whole, the conduct of all animated beings. In brief, one of the " Data" is that the nature of a man's actions cannot be properly determined unless we have previously considered the actions of the inferior animals and the causes of them. A common explanation of good and bad conduct is sought for and applied to the activities of all living creatures from the monad to the guinea-pig, and from the guinea-pig to man. It might not seem a very reasonable assertion that the value of the actions of a full-grown man is to be determined by the same tests as the value of his actions during infancy. But Mr. Spencer goes far beyond this. He links adult civilised man to the fishes and molluscs.

In infancy there are no distant views; the adult, on the other hand, as we have seen, tries actions by their relation to a remote consequence. He knows the result of certain actions; he can conjecture what will be the issue of many others. Here, whether evolution be true or not, we surely come to a distinctly new principle in the testing of conduct,—the ability man has to present to himself remote ideas and determine his action by a vision of good, that of others as well as his own; and of this principle Mr. Spencer makes a great deal. His scheme of human ethics hangs meanwhile on the foresight of consequences, the adjustment of acts to remote ends and the subordination of some desires to others. We would therefore expect him to insist on the essential distinction between the conduct of adult men and the conduct of animals. But no! He will have us go back to the beginnings of life and find the nature of duty and the basis of morality in the experiments of annelids and the discoveries of snails; and, passing on, we find the following illustration of the progress of morality and the nature of duty.

He contrasts a fish roaming about at hazard in search of food, able to detect it by sight or smell at short distances, now and again rushing away in alarm on the approach of a bigger fish, with an elephant, which detects food at relatively great distances by sight and smell, able to break off succulent or fruit-bearing branches, able to secure safety not only by flight, but, if necessary, by defence or attack, bringing into use tusks, trunk, and ponderous feet, able to use its trunk for projecting water over its body, for seizing a bough and sweeping flies from its back, or making signal sounds to alarm the herd.[1] We are taught to reckon the conduct of the elephant good as compared with that of the fish because it secures the balance of organic actions through a longer period, that is to say, greater duration of effective and pleasurable life. The actions of the elephant are good because they secure this, in the same sense and for the same reason as our conduct is good when it is elaborately adapted to our needs and prolongs our life. Of course quality of life is to be taken into account, and an oyster is not so good as a cuttle-fish, though it may live longer. We must consider the number of pleasure-giving activities that can be crowded into a given time;—so he says. Still the principle of all morality is to be found in the "conduct" of an elephant when it acts so as to preserve and prolong its life and tramples an enemy to the ground to save its young. And from the elephant, nay, from the ascidian to ourselves and our most complex conduct, there is not only continuity but identity of virtue. "The performance of every function is, in a sense, a moral obligation."[2]

Now, in view of what has already been said as to the ability of the developed human being to forecast

[1] Data, p. 12.   [2] Ibid., p. 76.

remote issues of his conduct and form a scheme of life, we have a right to ask whether Mr. Spencer is justified in limiting his definitions of good and bad in conduct so that they may apply alike to the lower animals and to men. Can we be content with a test that fits the mollusc, and seek no larger one when we come to ourselves? Is this moral philosophy? We may get an answer to such questions if we consider how the same method serves in another region.

A cathedral is of course built upon its foundation, and that foundation may be set very deep. It is just conceivable, indeed, that there may be as much building under as above ground. The nature and configuration of the site might make it necessary to go so far below the surface. When the antiquary came to examine such a cathedral it would be of interest to him to measure the depth of the foundation work, to note how the stones were dressed and jointed, to observe that below and above the same kind of stone had been used; and one still more intent on the pursuit of knowledge might go down to the stratum of rock on which the deep foundation rested. He would then be able to say much about the geological history of the site in remote ages. But how would all this investigation contribute to the knowledge of the superstructure, to a wise estimation of its purpose, acquaintance with its architectural style and its peculiar features? Would the explorer of the foundation be in any way helped by his researches underground in apprehending the beauty of the upper building and its adaptation to any special use? Suppose every stone of the lower courses were catalogued, the dimensions and weight of each carefully set down, would that determine in the least whether the building was a fine specimen or otherwise of its period, would any essential point be settled as to its character or end? If the explorer were to say: "Here in the foundation we see evidences of á design to go on raising walls indefinitely, and, whatever the other part of the building may be, its essential character is fixed here; you need look for no higher purpose than these courses exhibit;"—how would any sensible person regard him and his opinions? After poking about in his excavations he might resent the idea of worship as in any way connected with a building so begun, he might even assert that windows were not to be thought of, and that a roof was a sheer absurdity. It was perpendicular unbroken masonry that was the object. As for the carvings of pillar and capital, the tracery of windows, the tesselated pavement and richly wrought doorways, he might declare them mere inconsistent follies.

Now that is singularly like what Mr. Spencer has done in attempting a scientific exposition of universal conduct which shall explain the morality of man in terms not too large for the manners of the brutes. "Complete comprehension of conduct," he says, "is not to be obtained by contemplating the conduct of human beings only: we have to regard this as part of universal conduct. . . . And as in other cases so in this we must interpret the more developed by the less developed." Just as we can understand what morality is and how it came to be only when we have studied human conduct as a whole, so " fully to understand human conduct as a whole we must study it as a part of that larger whole constituted by the conduct of animate beings in general. . . . The conduct now shown by creatures of all orders is an outcome of the conduct which has brought life of every kind to its present height."[1] "We must interpret the more developed by the less developed;"—such is the principle: and it just means that, automatic pleasure-seeking being the law of the lowest animals, the highest duty of man is to return to it. There may be many departures from that principle between the protozoa and the highly moralised man. But continuity is complete, and the right idea of moral conduct begins to be grasped when we clearly see and aim at this final result.

2. *What does evolution command?*

Here, however, we cry halt in order to examine our author's notion of perfectly evolved conduct in relation to the strain of evolution. The task of constructing a system of ethics warranted to gratify the popular desire for a heaven has unfortunately made necessary a good deal of juggling with the laws of nature; and, in fact, our evolutionist has no sooner enunciated his doctrine of continuity between the conduct of animals and of

[1] Data, p. 7.

THE LOWER BIOLOGY.   139

men than he has to cast it overboard. With his eye always on the moralists who have gone before him, he has to frame an ideal, and it is to be found in a kind of conduct reached through physical evolution. His ideal of perfectly evolved conduct, that which will preserve the life of the individual as long as possible (for ever if possible,—that would be the only perfect kind), is such as will at the same time provide for the continuance of the race, and harm no other creature's life and activity. An automatism of this sort is desirable, nay, is necessary to happiness. In the perfectly moralised state of society there must be no war, no strife, no struggle for existence amongst men, nor even in the relations of men to the animals, and human moralisation is the attaining such a mode of activity.

Now, the alleged principle of continuity in conduct compels us to look back to the animals, and nothing can be clearer than that among them progress has been shaped by means of the struggle for existence, that is, not considering others outside their own circle, but contending with them. The more highly evolved creatures are those which were able to maintain themselves when placed side by side with others, whether those others suffered and perished or not. If anything has become fixed as a hereditary tendency in animated beings, one would say it is this determined egoism, qualified, if at all, by clannishness. Take civilised man, the highest specimen hitherto of evolved conduct; he destroys the larger carnivora and smaller rodents without mercy; he disputes with the aborigine of

America or Australia the possession of his territory, till the wild man has to give up the battle and life with it. Within society each fights for his own hand. One would say that under evolution if anything is to persist it is the hereditary law which this struggle going on during all past ages has established. It might even be maintained with reason that the struggle must increase, to result by-and-by in the development of the final fittest. And always the more evolved conduct, determining the evolutionary excellence of the better men, is their ability to gain victories over others by craft or strength, by hook or crook. If evolution leads to any conclusion as to morality it is, as Mr. Leslie Stephen says, that our duty is to be strong.

But what becomes of this law of nature, this principle of evolution in the "Data of Ethics?" It practically disappears. Mr. Spencer has to break totally with his theory that conduct is one in men and brutes. Evolution has produced carnivora which live by killing and are more highly evolved the greater their strength and ferocity. It has produced the elephant, which can attack enemies by using its tusks and ponderous feet. Such creatures are altruistic within the strictest limits of racial or even family sympathy. It has produced men who have all along cherished, in one form or other, the combative spirit. How, then, is this evolution by struggle and opposition ever to become an evolution of peace and *bonhomie?* How are we so to separate ourselves from the past as to think that our duty is to seek peace with all fellow-men, whatever their character, and with all our fellow-animals? Mr. Darwin was not so foolish as to dream of evolution taking such a turn. The struggle for existence was too evident to him. And Mr. Spencer ought, if we dare use the word, to have seen that evolution has nothing to do with morality.

Morality!—no indeed! Physical evolution is bent on something else. It is bent on converting matter and force to new uses. It is bent on peopling the earth to the limit of its supporting power, with every kind of animal and vegetable that can find means of existence. The organisms that emerge have to encounter hostile forces, and evolution, by furnishing them with new parts and functions, may aid them in the encounter. But with ideals of right and wrong, virtue and vice, it has nothing whatever to do. These ideas do not exist for it. Nature-evolution means the supply of varied forms and varied creatures; it means perpetual change and competition, until perchance the last pair fight for the last inch of standing-ground on the surface of a dissolving earth.

In his "First Principles"[1] Mr. Spencer has said that "there are not several kinds of evolution having certain traits in common, but one evolution going on everywhere after the same manner." The divisions into astronomic, geologic, biologic, psychologic, sociologic, "are mere conventional groupings," and "evolution is not one in principle only but one in fact,—and this holds uniformly regardless of the size of the aggregate." Precisely: but, if this be so, what matters it to show

[1] Page 545.

how here and there creatures urged on by forces which they cannot resist, helped or hindered by chance differentiations, bent on satisfying their own needs, yet under an inherited necessity of conserving the race to which they belong, sometimes make way for each other as they pass on to seek happiness more or less remote? There is no morality here, but an accident of time, place, circumstance. The law of life or vital progress is not the deferring now and again to some or helping a few who belong to a favoured circle. No evolutionary obligation can be affirmed regarding these subordinate details. The great unwavering law of life is,—Live each according to your fashion; go on living as long as you can; enjoy whenever you can; exercise every faculty and avoid every perceived danger; the longer you are able to do this, whether by what is called virtuous or what is called vicious action, the more evolved is your conduct,—the better an animal you are. To this and this only is it possible to come as a rule of vital activity if we consider evolution as one series of physical changes and estimate the higher development by the lower. All altruism, in short, is a measure of death, since it checks the free play of individual action. According to any physical theory of evolution the sole ethical rule is that stated by Mr. Darwin:—"Multiply, vary, let the strongest live and the weakest die."[4]

[1] Origin of Species, sixth edition, p. 234.

THE LOWER BIOLOGY. 143

3. *No ghost, no duty.*

We return, however, to the assumption, strangely at variance with all this, that while the lower animals make it their business to live as long as they can and are highly evolved in proportion as they succeed, needing no ethical rules, man, whose conduct is continuous with theirs, whose great aim is precisely the same, has to be bothered with moral questions and philosophies, worried with adjustments between altruism and egoism, between remote and immediate enjoyment. We return, in short, to the attempt of Mr. Spencer to fill up his imaginary vacuum. And here, on the way to discover that the sense of obligation is a temporary intrusion, useful more or less for the present stage, but destined to fade into thin air,—here we come to the matter of religion, its nature and use.

Religion: yes, that is a great obstinate fact. And if we re-open the "Data of Ethics" and inquire concerning it, we find the history of the religious sanction to be after this manner:—" In all but the rudest groups, the double of a deceased man, propitiated at death and afterwards, is conceived as able to injure the survivors. Consequently, as fast as the ghost-theory becomes established and definite there grows up a check on immediate satisfaction of the desires, a check constituted by ideas of the evils which ghosts may inflict if offended; and when political headship gets settled, and the ghosts of dead chiefs, thought of as more powerful and more relentless than other ghosts, are specially dreaded, there begins to take shape the form of restraint distinguished as religious. . . . As the chief gains predominance the killing of enemies becomes a political duty; and as the anger of the dead chief comes to be dreaded the killing of enemies becomes a religious duty. . . . . The divine injunctions, originally traditions of the dead king's will, mainly refer to the destruction of peoples with whom he was at enmity, and divine anger or approval are conceived as determined by the degrees in which subjection to him is shown, directly by worship and indirectly by fulfilling these injunctions." So far on page 116 of the "Data." But on page 119 we read:— "The sinfulness of breaking a divine injunction was universally at one time, and is still by many, held to consist in the disobedience to God rather than in the deliberate entailing of injury; and even now it is a common belief that acts are right only if performed in conscious fulfilment of the divine will."

Now, apart from the question—by no means a trifling one—how far and in what sense these representations of religious feeling are true, there is at any rate a vast interval of development between the religious ideas set forth in the two quotations. In the first, allowing it, for the sake of argument, to pass meanwhile, we have the most primitive notion of religious "duty" that could well be conceived; in the second we have a high spiritual loyalty described, a loyalty which leads to the love of enemies, an "altruism" at least as fine as that of the "Data of Ethics," and a moral strength which defies superstitious fears. The one condition is that of the savage, the other that of such a man as Faraday or Clerk Maxwell. Continuity is again assumed, however, and not continuity alone, but essential identity.

This belief in supernatural beings—although an utter falsity—was useful in maintaining a feeling of obligation; it was a conception "potent over undeveloped minds," and, besides, the religious has been one of the lower classes of feelings and restraints by which are "maintained the conditions under which the higher feelings and restraints," that is to say, those of scientific morality, "evolve."[1] In other words, no ghost, no duty; no religion, no moral restraint; no God, no civilisation. The authority of human law has been one necessary thing; the authority of a guess at supernatural beings has been another necessary thing. Now, however, both are to disappear; moralisation takes the field, and how that works we shall by-and-by learn.

Here, first, there is a question of interest which may be suggested for the consideration of evolutionists,— How is it that among the inferior animals there is no trace of embryonic religion? If human religion is a delusion, a mere "ghost-theory," it seems remarkable that these animals, which are popularly supposed to have less intelligence than men, should have remained absolutely free from the preposterous dream. No dog believes that his old master "walks" or that a bigger dog, now in the shades, demands an offering of bone which must be laid for it in an appropriate place with accompanying

[1] Data, pp. 120, 121.

howls and grovelling in the dust. We rise from the undeluded dog, the undeluded monkey to man—and behold! so strangely does his higher intelligence work that he not only believes in ghosts but is helped by the belief. Mr. Spencer does not venture into the lowest groups of human beings but stays in those which are "all but lowest" when he is searching for the germ of religion. Why did he not go further? Does continuity cease here again and leave another gap—with the fools on this side and the wise generations on the other, the creatures whom it was no wonder Æsop studied, since they were sagacious enough to be content with nature and imagined no supernatural absurdities?

And there is another question more imperatively demanding consideration and reply. Does evolution work with delusions and dreams; are fancies and superstitions just as useful in producing varieties of life, physical, mental, social, as unquestionable facts? A point like this does really make the "plain reasonable person" rub his eyes and inquire whether he too sees visions about. Religion began with ghosts, simple and compound. If you persist in tracing its germ, that can only be found by the believer in continuity in the start of an ape when a shadow fell suddenly across him or a cry woke him from sleep. But the plain truth is that evolution ought to prevent its creatures from becoming subject to vanity. It must be against every individual, simian or human, that is nervous and apt to start at shadows, much more against every race of beings that persist in attributing existence and power to what has no reality. It is evident that notions of ghosts and of obligation to them could never be of the least use to a savage if ghost there was none, and the argument of the "Data of Ethics," proceeding on the basis that real increase of life and happiness is secured by all changes and adaptations, must imply that ghosts exist and have the power of blessing and cursing.

By the notion he formed of a dead chief the savage was deterred from something he might have done or urged to something he would not otherwise have done. Now he deprived himself of food which he foolishly offered in sacrifice, and, at another time, he felt constrained to fight when there was not the least occasion. Evolution must have played tricks of one sort or another, and the progress of the human race has been conditioned by those tricks. Like many other points in the discussion, this invites more comment than there is space for; but it is quite clear that a tribe which did not believe in ghosts, did not care about dead ancestors or their imaginary whims, being too practical for that sort of thing, would have more food, fewer quarrels, and generally speaking, a better time—the all-important matter—than another which cultivated religion. Will Mr. Spencer tell us how and why evolution favoured the latter and enabled it to swallow up the former? Why were the superstitious folk not weeded out by the matter-of-fact forces of nature? How came about the development of the ghost-cult—the belief always growing in bigger and bigger ghosts, national ghosts, whole settlements of ghosts? Surely there was always a possibility of putting their existence to the proof, and as intellect became more keen and competent why were the tests not applied? Evolution being for common-sense should have suppressed the fools who misspent time and offerings and their own blood, cutting themselves with knives in honour of Baal, throwing themselves under the wheels of Jagganath. How, then, has it been possible for superstition to grow and spread and take so many luxuriant forms?

But our author, holding that evolution has played tricks with men, lightly assuming that it has made for beliefs which have no foundation, has encouraged them and used them to good purpose, carries out his theory to its logical conclusion. With long and sinuous reasoning he labours to assure us that the purest form of monotheism or Christianity is a growth from the ghost-theory, a persistent delusion. Since there are no ghosts, therefore there is no God, at least in any sense accepted since men began to believe: all the notions we now have of a Supreme Being, intelligent, righteous, loving, true, are the product of primitive ghost-fancies, and are worth as much or as little. So he comes to his great object as an ethical teacher, the banishing of these theological conceptions in order that scientific morality, otherwise habit, otherwise automatic pleasure-seeking, may have the field to itself.

By means of an illustration let us sift the treatment of religion by Mr. Spencer, its fairness and logic. Take a primitive man dwelling by the shore of some Pacific or Atlantic of prehistoric time, one of those men whose belief in the hovering shades of deceased ancestors is said to be the root of our belief in God. This man made for himself a dug-out canoe. His ability to use the material provided by nature, his intelligence, activity, and skill served him so far, but no farther. By means of his rude hollowed log he could cross the river at whose mouth he dwelt, and even venture in search of fish a little way upon the great flood that seemed to end his world on one side. Exactly parallel to his notions of shadowy beings and of the duties he owed them were his notions of the universe and his ability to use nature. The results he attained in the shape of canoe, bone fish-hooks, and clumsy net were on much the same level, it would seem, as his achievements in the way of morality, social organisation, faith in the supernatural. But with the progress of intelligence and industrial skill, with repeated experiments ending in new discoveries and clearer knowledge, it became possible for man to construct a ship, to make a compass and chronometer, to guide his course by observation of sun, moon, and stars, and so reach a distant shore; and in process of time we have the steam-vessel of 5000 tons burden, capable of conveying a thousand passengers across the globe to lands the savage never imagined. Now it would seem supremely absurd to charge Mr. Spencer with asserting that the steamship cannot bring us to a land beyond the range of vision because in his dug-out canoe the savage could not cross the ocean. And yet when we apply to this case his fixed principle of interpreting the more developed by the less developed the conclusion can only be that the steamship, though it may bear us out to sea, cannot enable us to land on any unseen shore. What was a *terra incognita* to the primeval man must be a *terra incognita* to us, will for ever remain a *terra incognita*. Improve your methods of navigation as you will, use chart and compass, chronometer and sextant, adapt the steam-engine to propel your vessel, drive her ahead against storm and tide; always the limit of human achievement is determined by the first success. There is a land beyond the great ocean no doubt, a something of which we have adumbrations. But he who steps on board a vessel at Liverpool or London in expectation of reaching a shore vaguely spoken of as the antipodes, named even as Australia or New Zealand, is a dreamer. That trans-oceanic region is inscrutable, beyond the power of vision to see or logic to prove or navigation to reach. The steamship, immense as the skill and ingenuity expended on it have been, is a useless conceit, a moving exhibition of human folly.

The original barbarian feared the great water and never sought to pass beyond the creek or river-mouth beside which he was born. As the forest was full of mystery and danger, so was the sea; and parallel with this feeling were those of religious awe, belief in divine or supernatural beings. He was limited, ignorant, the prey of fears. As in his poor dug-out canoe he could paddle about a little and catch food, so in his "vague perception of mystery" he had a small experience of that fundamental verity which in its developed and scientific form now-a-days is "the recognition of inscrutableness." Now, says Mr. Spencer, if you think you can venture across high seas of truth and arrive at any unseen continent of life because you have a bigger and more elaborate vessel you are under a delusion. The only "verity" in this evolved religion of yours is the recognition of the sea as a great deep. Elaborate theology is of no more value as a means of ascertaining truth than the imaginations of the savage. The Eternal cannot be known.

4. *The moral imperative of — Gaster.*

It may seem almost incredible that one who assigns to religion an essential part in the education of the race, declares that without it the conditions of moralisation could never have been reached and affirms that it has had "the all-essential office of preventing men from being wholly absorbed in the relative and immediate,"[1] should be quite ready to dismiss it as of no value in the morals of the future, and should trust the evolution which has produced it and found it indispensable to sweep it away as a basis of obligation and a motive of progress. This, in the ethical region, would seem equivalent to a notion that animal life, hitherto dependent on oxygen, is about to dispense with that element, while there is apparently as much need as ever for it and no sign that evolution demands the change. We might think that the still further puri-

[1] First Principles, p. 101.

fication of religion from all falsehood and superstition, its establishment as the secure basis of individual and social ethics, are the needs of our time which a moralist ought to have in view. Since, at all events, the immense majority of people are by no means at the stage where the original restraints of religion and law can be safely set aside and any confirmed habit of genial altruism making for egoistic happiness can be relied upon, we might have expected that Mr. Spencer would set himself rather to "strengthen the things that remain" than to encourage an experiment which the past does not commend and urge a course which the merest glance might show him to be full of peril. But his task, once undertaken under the strange delusion that there is a "vacuum," and the stranger delusion still that he can do something to fill it up, is carried on with at least a show of serene self-complacency. He has admitted that religion, human law, and public opinion have to do with the sense of obligation as it is still acknowledged by man. But he labours to prove that there is a kind of obligation, quite apart from religion and human law and public opinion, fitted to serve the end of keeping things going, so to speak, when the other restraints and sanctions disappear;—itself of a kind which will easily merge in the automatism that is finally to hold the field of ethics.

Taking an elementary case in which obligation and morality arise, we have the following,[1] as clear if not as elegant a statement of Mr. Spencer's theory as can

[1] Data, p. 159.

well be desired: "Before the gullet swallows the jaws must lay hold; before the jaws tear out and bring within grasp of the gullet a piece fit for swallowing there must be that co-operation of limbs and senses required for killing the prey; before this co-operation can take place there needs be much longer co-operation constituting the chase, and even before this there must be persistent activities of limbs, eyes and nose, in seeking prey. The pleasure attending each set of acts, while making possible the pleasure attending the set of acts which follows, is joined with a representation of this subsequent set of acts and its pleasure, and of the others which succeed in order; so that along with the feelings accompanying the search for prey are partially aroused the feelings accompanying the actual chase, the actual destruction, the actual devouring and the eventual satisfaction of appetite." A "fact" here is "that the use of each set of means in due order constitutes an obligation. Maintenance of its life being regarded as the end of its conduct, the creature is obliged to use in succession the means of finding prey, the means of catching prey, the means of killing prey, the means of devouring prey." "The relations between means and ends thus traced . . . hold true of human conduct up even to its highest forms."[1] So the elaborate arrangements of business are made to prove that "observance of moral principles is fulfilment of certain general conditions to the successful carrying on of special activities."[2] If you ask why a trader ought to keep his engagements

[1] Data, p. 160.   [2] Ibid., p. 162.

with creditors the answer is as follows: "That the trader may prosper"—a necessity which is taken for granted, like many other things—"he must not only keep his books correctly, but must pay those he employs according to agreement, and must meet his engagements with creditors. . . . May we not infer," proceeds Mr. Spencer, "that though conformity to moral requirements precedes in imperativeness conformity to other requirements, yet this imperativeness" —that called moral—"arises from the fact that fulfilment of the other requirements, by self or others or both, is thus furthered?" Mr. Spencer says, "May we not infer?" Of course, since it is necessary to his scheme to infer, he may. Who hinders? But will he persuade any sane persons that he has here a moral scheme? That is quite another affair. It is your duty to meet engagements with creditors. Why? Not because a man should be faithful to his promises, just, honourable; not because his relation to the eternal order of the universe binds him here, ordains that he shall be free in soul and conscience only by keeping in the line of truth, righteousness, and honour: not at all; but because his welfare, his "gratification," the filling of his belly, in fact, requires that moral engagements should be met. So, as Carlyle says, the stomach and its appurtenances are the active source and mainstay of moral principle.

The audacious synthesis of this stage is finally formulated in the words:—" Understanding their relative positions, those ethical systems which make virtue, right, obligation, the cardinal aims, are seen to be complementary to those ethical systems which make welfare, pleasure, happiness, the cardinal aims." Complementary: is that just the right word? Reason, conscience, justice, purity, truth, complementary to the scheme of self-pleasing qualified by easy altruism! You may guide yourself by "innate perceptions of right, duly enlightened and made precise by analytic intelligence"[1]—that is, if you can, if you have the innate perceptions and the precise analytic intelligence. But you have always to be on your guard lest you attribute too much importance to them. They are guides "proximately supreme." The "ultimately supreme end is happiness special and general"—the gratification of *Gaster* and his appurtenances. True, we have much talk about the "highest life," the "ideal form of being," "perfection or excellence of nature." The "theological theory" is, in order to disarm prejudice, allowed to contain a part of truth. You have but to substitute "for the divine will, supposed to be supernaturally revealed, the naturally revealed end towards which the Power manifested throughout evolution works"—in short, you have but to turn out theology, neck and heels, and religion, what is left of it, remains a useful complement of the happiness scheme. We cannot but thank Mr. Spencer for this valuable concession. Observe, the obligation underlying every conception of ethics, according to him, is egoistic—the obligation of a man to find, first and chiefly, the food and drink that

[1] Data, p. 173.

give him pleasure, and, thereafter, cunningly adapt himself to other people so that they will not interfere with the satisfaction of his appetites. The ideal life of man rises in no degree above that of a singing-bird or a peacock. Obligation in either case is precisely the same in its nature. And if man goes far about in attempting to secure the fulfilment of his cravings, enters into social relations which give him a deal of trouble, cultivates art, writes books, constructs moral schemes and ideals, ponders the "Data of Ethics,"—why, the greater fool he! If he only knew it, evolution has nothing better to give him than happiness, and cannot ensure that, when he has mastered the Synthetic Philosophy and found the equilibrium of perfect life, he will enjoy his existence more than the savage in a primeval forest.

Against this it seems needless to argue at further length. The statement of the case is sufficient to refute the theory of obligation. There could have been no pursuit of moral greatness or spiritual beauty if morality has the character ascribed to it in the "Data of Ethics." A shorter way would have been found to the "ultimate end" of happiness. The history of the human race remains unexplained in Mr. Spencer's philosophy, for the object of human "progress" would have been reached without those long investigations, those elaborate sciences, those innumerable experiments in government and religion, all of which have, so far from aiding, only hindered the attainment of the highest good. The ultimate pleasure spoken of is so purely physical in its nature, the perfect life by which it is to be reached is on so low and earthly a level, that the achievement of it would only put a fool's cap on human history.

5. *Man meddling with evolution.*

How can the evolutionist affirm that progress which has been conditioned all along by theological beliefs of one sort or another will continue up to the full height of possibility after belief in the Living God has been sent to join astrology and divination? Evolution is one, we have been told, and advances by the same law from age to age. Each new force coming into action has the same source, the same justification—necessity. But if all the forces that spring from belief in the supernatural are to cease, will morality be the same, will there remain any possibility of forecasting evolution? Is it not as if the sense of sight were to be lost and the development completely arrested that has been due to it? In either case would it not be equally absurd to predict any future for the human race at all? Whatever religion may have been in its origin,— whether a dream of ignorance, a guess of fear, or something springing of necessity from the contact of mind with a higher mind revealed in nature and in itself—it has, by admission of the scientific examiner, played no small part in the evolution of men. Without the religions of our race the whole human story would have been entirely different, if indeed it could have been at all.

> "Which has not taught weak wills how much they can?
> Which has not fall'n on the dry heart like rain?
> Which has not cried to sunk, self-weary man :
>   Thou must be born again?"

Each idea, each hope, fear, sanction which, having the same origin as man himself, has powerfully affected his action in the past was indispensable. The guidance religion gives to human conduct has been necessary. How is an evolutionist to explain that away and boldly predict that we shall do better without it?

Here we would seem to have tracked Mr. Spencer and his Synthetic Philosophy into a *cul-de-sac*. But no! A most extraordinary assertion to come from an evolutionist is made in order to show that all the help religion has given, as well as other kinds of help essential hitherto to progress, may be dispensed with and abandoned and the whole business still go merrily forward. Did we dream for a moment that there was an evolutionary necessity for the faith of God, belief in eternal justice, responsibility to a Judge who will do right, love to One whose promises kindle hope, whose character commands reverence and admiration? That was our unfortunate mistake. Mr. Spencer can see differences where to the simple-minded person, "not apt," as Mr. Arnold says, "for fine distinctions," there are none. We have to learn that under evolution there are, as products of human thought and enterprise, certain ideas, sanctions, consequences of action that are factitious—not natural, not according to the true course of things, but manufactured, got up for a purpose.

THE LOWER BIOLOGY.

We have heard of three "controls," the political, the religious, and the social, within which "the moral control evolves." What is our surprise to discover that these "controls" depend entirely on that which is "factitious"! They have "evolved with the evolution of society"[1] because they were "necessary under the conditions" and are "in the main congruous with each other," but the plain truth about them is that they are dependent on "factitious evil consequences;" the results of disobedience under any one of the three—a legal penalty, a supernatural punishment, a social reprobation"—results "more vividly conceived," and therefore more "potent over undeveloped minds" than those "which, in the course of things" (that is, according to necessitarian evolution), "actions naturally entail," are "incidental rather than necessary."[2] But the results which constitute the only true moral control, while they may happen to coincide here and there with the others, are not to be confounded with them. On the one hand are the extrinsic, superposed, factitious consequences; on the other are the natural, intrinsic, necessary consequences. The moral motive "is constituted by representations of consequences which the acts naturally produce."[3]

There is here a distinction which is not to be denied. It is quite true that "one who is morally prompted to fight against a social evil" may have "neither material benefit nor popular applause before his mind"—the "factitious" consequences—"but only the mischiefs he

[1] Data, p. 119.   [2] Ibid., p. 120.   [3] Ibid., p. 121.

seeks to remove and the increased well-being which will follow their removal."[1] Taking for granted a limited atheistical notion of morality, one may allow that the sense of this distinction marks a highly moral state of mind. But from the point of view of the Synthetic Philosophy the distinction between extrinsic and intrinsic—as if these terms were in any sense equivalent to unnatural and natural—appears astonishing and incomprehensible. It may be true that the moral deterrent from murder is a representation of certain results —" the infliction of the death agony on the victim, the destruction of all his possibilities of happiness, the entailed sufferings to his belongings "[2]—that this deterrent is different in kind from the fear of hanging, or of torture in hell, or of the horror and hatred excited in fellow-men. But the distinction is not one that monistic evolution admits. If evolution has produced government and law, it has produced the gallows; if it has produced belief in ghosts, it has produced the fear of hell; if it has produced society, it has produced the horror and disgrace which light on the murderer. Talk of the headsman's block and axe or their modern substitute the gallows as not natural or necessary! Mr. Spencer appears to entertain the notion that while nature and evolution are at work producing legitimate and true effects man is at work for his part counter to nature, or at least apart from nature. When he forms a society, believes in a religion, obeys a chief, he interferes with evolution, and all the results of his action

[1] Data, p. 121.   [2] Ibid., p. 120.

are "factitious." In brief, he is really defying evolution. Man, the product of nature, every organ and faculty, every art and science of his equally a result of evolution, does something under that supreme control, and yet it is not a "natural necessary product," it is not upon the same level as some consequence which follows evil-doing without human intervention. A wild beast may kill a man, and that we suppose is natural; a ruler orders him to the gallows, and that is a "factitious evil." The fear of the wild beast's claws and teeth is a moral motive, but the fear of the judge and what he may order has nothing to do with morality; for the moral motive here, because it suits Mr. Spencer to say so, is to be distinguished from the political and social and religious motives that are purely "incidental, collateral, non-necessary."

Where are we in this chaos? When, under British law, a poisoner is sent to the gallows, is that not as much a fact, an evolutionary fact, a fact of the nature and course of things taken as a whole as any internal reflection upon "the death-agony of the victim, the destruction of his happiness, the sufferings of his belongings?" If Mr. Spencer says that arrest and conviction do not always follow, will he affirm that his "natural necessary" feelings always exist, or will he tell us how often they arise beforehand to *prevent* murder? Suppose a murderer is clever enough to kill his victim without pain, suppose the latter is a very old person, and has no relations who will be affected by his death— where is there any chance for those deterrents which Mr.

L

Spencer declares to be alone moral, on which he relies for the suppression of murder when the theologian's hell and the ruler's gallows have departed and left a "vacuum"? In that case, it is to be supposed, the other representations present to the mind of the murderer that he will possess himself of his victim's hoard and live happily ever after, may properly control his action.

But the judge and jury, the hangman and the rope, are certainly a part of the course of things, more actual than those mental reflections on which Mr. Spencer relies. Whatever sort of government uses the machinery of law, whether it is used justly or unjustly, it must be reckoned with, and conduct is good or bad in relation to it. Evolutionary science can no more argue that social reprobation is unnatural and incidental than that society itself is so. If the opinions of other people are to be placed outside the category of moral deterrents, what becomes of altruism? Notwithstanding all his talk about the social organism, Mr. Spencer had better avow himself an out and out individualist: then he might say plainly that hanging is immoral, instead of leaving us to come at his belief on that point by a process of inference. As it is we arrive at the conclusion that when the "Data of Ethics" becomes the basis of a legal code there will be an entirely new way of dealing with murderers and thieves. Instead of inquiring whether the accused was guilty, as we say, of a certain act declared by law to be a crime, we shall have to consider his feelings and family circumstances, his calculation of results and the degree in which he sought to lessen his victim's pain. Then we may have to reward the man rather than punish him.

It must be allowed that the attempt to discredit the controls which have been of so much use in the past by the introduction of the theory of the factitious is a complete failure. Human government and social reprobation stand as evolutionary facts and cannot be got rid of. Religion rests on a foundation at least as firm: and if Mr. Spencer had been wise he would not only have made this clear but done his utmost to emphasise the importance of religion and add to its power. Without it he is trusting to influences and tendencies utterly inadequate. See how poor a hope it is. Human choice, on which dependence is at present placed and will be for thousands of years, is gradually to merge in habit automatically infallible. At the long last, without religion, without government or any control by popular opinion, each shall be so moralised that the will may go to sleep. People shall be good as naturally and spontaneously as they breathe or speak. All this is to come if we only give up "factitious" deterrents from wrong-doing and allow ourselves to be drawn on by those moral motives which, if we yield to them, are sure to give us the highest pleasure and so vindicate their authority.

6. *The mountain barrier.*

Convinced as Mr. Spencer is that the changes which have led hitherto towards the perfect life will continue to go on till the perfect life is attained, irrational though he declares it to be to doubt the evolution of humanity, he has to confess that as yet, under the present imperfect conditions of society, perfect or ideal life is an impossibility for any one. Mankind as a whole is in the groove of imperfection, active there, finding an immense amount of pleasure there, much of it unquestionably of an immoral kind. Mental inertia, the forces of heredity and habit, the struggle for existence, the pleasures that are purely personal all co-operate towards keeping it in this groove. Each individual by his close connection with others, as well as by his own inherited tendencies, finds it difficult to shift into a better. Nor is there any reason to suppose that, within his own lifetime, he shall be able so to settle himself and those around him in a way more nearly approaching the perfect that the result would repay the effort. Here therefore is the mountain barrier between us and Utopia; and the question is, Can it be crossed? So long as religion remains a force, and by its great ideas of responsibility and immortality, its sublime inspirations, continues to guide the energy of man, there might seem to be hope. It is not merely, as Mr. Spencer tries to make it, a system of deterrents frightening credulous people by the fear of hell; it supplies mighty impulses and great ambitions for the enthusiastic. Hitherto it has done much; but it is to decay, and yet the mountain barrier is to be crossed.

It would be right here to press for an answer to the question how it comes to pass that while the ideal life is unattainable by any one, the notion of it can be framed, how indeed there can be any ideal, either for the individual or for society. Suppose we affirm that evolution, after it has urged life along a certain line for some time, is in the way of leaving off short of the "type" and beginning to guide energy in another direction? Suppose we maintain that, after favouring altruism for a long series of years, evolution will suddenly, under conditions that may easily be anticipated, decide for physical strength and the law that might is to be right, making the relations of men to each other throughout the world like those of animals in a forest? Will Mr. Spencer or any evolutionist declare that change to be impossible? There would be a vast amount of bloodshed; nine-tenths of the human race might disappear; but this is no difficulty. Nature cares no more for the good man than for the strong. The thing is possible, in a sense probable. Where, then, is the ideal discoursed of in the "Data"?

Under the theory which governs Mr. Spencer's philosophy nothing is certain but what is. And any one who studies the synthetic scheme for a day with the least attention will be sure to discover that. Ideals, remote possibilities, the representation and re-representation of consequences are all beside the mark. Long-drawn arguments and bewildering discussions of inevitable adaptations and progress sure to come can never in the least obscure the main issue to one who sees what is implied in the contention that religion has passed away and left a vacuum. If for a time certain inconvenient laws of society and remnants of superstition keep things going in something like the old groove, it can only be till the veil is withdrawn entirely from the naked truth, and men, confessing that they are like the beasts that perish, apply themselves with the same decision and straightforwardness as the beasts to the main business of life.

But suppose the ideal state of society to be credibly made out, the point is to commend it to those who are settled in the un-ideal, wedded to the un-ideal; how, in short, to get the human caravan to move.

"There is no kind of activity, consistent with maintenance of life, which will not become a source of pleasure if continued; pleasure therefore will eventually accompany every mode of action demanded by social conditions."[1] Again: "It was pointed out that, supposing them to be consistent with continuance of life, there are no activities which may not become sources of pleasure, if surrounding conditions require persistence in them. And here it is to be added . . . that if the conditions require any class of activities to be relatively great, there will arise a relatively great pleasure accompanying that class of activities."[2] Such is the principle on which we are asked to rely. In other words, being obliged to move along in a certain rut, move in it long enough and you will come to like it. This and this alone from first to last of the "Data of Ethics" will be found as the infallible basis of moralisation and of hope.

[1] Data, p. 186. [2] Ibid., p. 249.

Well, does this animate the would-be believer? Society has perhaps made him a drudge, a hewer of wood and drawer of water. The doing of that work is consistent with maintenance of life so far that he gets coarse food for hard labour. Is it comforting to know that if he goes on long enough in the rut he will come to like it; that by the time his limbs are stiff with rheumatism and his mind is completely absorbed in daily toil he will be a happy man? What a solace for the toiler in such a faith! And, let it be added, what a defence for the tyrants who shall rule in the coming social slavery! Mr. Spencer may in his sweet and simple terms declare that this principle is to be taken in connection with the other that " the type of nature to which the highest social life affords a sphere such that every faculty has its due amount, and no more than its due amount, of gratification, is the type of nature towards which progress cannot cease until it is reached." To be sure:—and this wonderful type will be reached ten thousand generations hence. Meanwhile for all who bear the burdens, endure the tyranny, groan and sweat under the load of life, the solace is that their activity will become a source of pleasure if continued; for the mass of mankind constituting the " sacrificed classes " with no hope of seeing the illimitably distant ideal age the gospel is that they have but to endure a little longer, and still a little longer, and they will become happy in their servitude and chains. Will that sweeten their prospect? Will that " fill up the vacuum "? Will it keep in check the volcanic forces of revolution?

But the strange thing is that it is expected to do far more. It is on this and nothing else that Mr. Spencer relies to keep the human caravan moving on the right line, so that by-and-by the mountain barrier may be crossed. Habit gradually establishing itself till it becomes a means of happiness is to lead us on ; independently of all sense of duty or obligation, we shall go forward under this magical impulse, advancing towards the remote ideal. Nothing else is needed. We might have thought that if habit is supreme, and, persisted in long enough, becomes pleasurable, all progress would terminate when the imaginary hopes kindled by religion died out. One would have been almost inclined to prophesy that this pessimistic conclusion would sum up the results of the Synthetic Philosophy. Setting out with a qualified optimism as a working theory, Mr. Spencer might have been expected to end with the statement that humanity is now, in the weary wisdom of philosophic age, settling itself down by the fireside in its arm-chair to doze out its last days, forgetting if it can the vain conflicts of thousands of years. But we are mistaken. Still we hear of that ideal " towards which progress cannot cease till it is reached." Beyond the high mountain range lies the happy valley, and habit, which if continued long enough always gives happiness, is the rut in which motion is to continue, while the desire for happiness which habit gives is the motive-force bringing us to the delightful land. Is this not perspicuous ? The critic cannot help it.

Under the influence of religion and the political and social beliefs that somehow were useful to undeveloped man there has been a great deal of stir and conflict in human history. We attribute to these much of our intellectual progress, as we call it, and by them we have been urged to varied activities making necessary a complex morality. But the main thing all along has been happiness. Beneath all that was done and suffered for the sake of religion, all that was aimed at in government and allowed or frowned upon by public opinion, there was the fact, too dimly perceived by far, that happiness is the one thing needful. Did men make much of fearing God and honouring the king? What they really wanted was happiness; and those were roundabout ways of getting at it. Did they submit to Mrs. Grundy or rebel against her? They may have supposed weakly that there was some necessity in the former case, and in the latter that they were actuated by principle; but in reality it was the instinctive desire for happiness that was at the bottom of what they did. In the course of its history every nation has had revolutions and wars. Sometimes it was the injustice of government, sometimes a religious motive that led to those violent changes. But it was happiness that was the real desideratum, and yet if anything has been made clear it is that increase of happiness was never proportioned to the effort. The nations would have done immensely better for themselves to go on in the rut in which they were at any given time till by continuing in it their activities became pleasureable. They should have adapted themselves, in short, to their circumstances and avoided militarism of every kind as their hell. Now we have come to see the truth as to these things. We see that theological ideas only interfered with the real progress of the race, substituting factitious consequences for those which are natural. We see that government and public opinion keep men from the things best worth having, alone worth having. Now with our eyes open we set aside those unfortunate mistakes and delusions of undeveloped humanity and give ourselves up to the true principle of progress which happily during the many centuries of blundering has kept its hold of our nature; now we abandon ourselves to the imperative obligation of giving our faculties "their due amount of gratification."

> Let duty, virtue, law, religion die,
> We have at length the true morality.

Mr. Spencer claims to have argued on purely natural grounds from what has been to what shall be. He has shown us the theoretically perfect life of men in society to which evolution is bound to bring them. And what is our present duty; how are we to escape the perplexities in ethical speculation and in life by which many have been bewildered? Always yielding ourselves to pleasant habits we are to keep in view the important idea of "the least wrong." That is all we can achieve meanwhile on the way to the ideal. The absolutely right is in the air, was never realised or seen.

But the least wrong, what gives the least amount of pain, since pain in this imperfect state there must unfortunately be, let us aim at that, decide for that. The long discipline and high ardour of life, the providential stress, the sacred burdens laid on us for the training of our spirits—all these disappear. We are to settle ourselves into the least wrong, and that will bring us to the perfectly right.

So the new career is before us. The vacuum is filled. For fear of God there is avoidance of pain. For holiness there is hedonism. For the quest of truth there is acceptance of habit. For the stir of progress and the cry—

> "One crowded hour of glorious life
> Is worth an age without a name,"

there is the easier *rôle*—

> "Eating the lotos day by day,
>   To watch the crisping ripples on the beach
> And tender curving lines of creamy spray,
>   To lend our hearts and spirits wholly
> To the influence of mild-minded melancholy;
>   To muse and brood and live again in memory,
> With those old faces of our infancy
> Heap'd over with a mound of grass,
> Two handfuls of white dust, shut in an urn of brass!"

7. *The deep of scientific doubt.*

There is a persistent undercurrent of suggestion throughout the whole of the "Data of Ethics" that man cannot be good unless he is prosperous. The morality is that of a well-to-do race without anxiety or hardship, reaping the easily won harvests of a propitious world. We seem, all the time, to be hearing the voice of the "Northern Farmer—new style":—

"Tis'n them as 'as munny as breäks into 'ouses an' steäls,
Them as 'as coäts to their backs an' taäkes their regular meäls.
Noä, but it's them as niver knaws wheer a meäl's to be 'ad;
Taäke my word for it, Sammy, the poor in a loomp is bad."

The ideal of which we are told so much is unapproachable by those who are not possessed of good means; it is unattainable unless Nature so favours the coming race as to change her harshness into generosity, sheathe her weapons of offence and leave her happy children to their lotos-eating and automatic innocence. This is a large expectation, the absurdity of which Mr. Spencer cannot fail to have seen; but if we look for any treatment of the grave question of man's relation to nature, his dependence on its supplies, the certainty that he will always have to struggle with natural forces and that population will increase up to the limit of food production, we shall find nothing of the sort. Increase of heterogeneity is Mr. Spencer's way of stating progress. The maximum of heterogeneity is the high-water-mark of evolution. Plainly, then, increase of population, increase and complexity of struggle are essential conditions of man's evolutionary progress, and a scheme of moralisation which quietly ignores them cannot claim to be based on evolutionary science. Of course it is *absolute* Ethics, of which the "Data" are laid down for us, but here the fact comes out that the absolute state can never exist on this earth, in plain English the ethics are those of an impossible Utopia.

We are told of an evolution of humanity; we ought to be told also of an evolution of nature keeping pace with human development, or rather preceding it, holding out continually the hope of greater ease and prosperity, making larger provision to meet the larger wants of men. Now Mr. Spencer has not dared, in the whole course of the "Data," to confess that he sees no prospect of nature adjusting itself in this way to the needs of humanity, he has not dared to make a confession which would have shown him bound in the chains of a wretched pessimism. Our author much dislikes being classed with Jeremy Bentham and the Utilitarians; but he came from that camp, and would have done well to remain there; for the limitation of the Utilitarian was his safety, and, so long as Evolution was not in all men's mouths, the greatest happiness formula was a neat enough little recipe. But there came that wonderful thought, Evolution; it was a revelation, it was to explain everything, and it has explained away Utilitarianism, the older sort and Mr. Spencer's as well. The expansion has been ruin. Happiness-ethic is an impossibility, a contradiction in terms. All you can get is "a science of health," and, dismissing the moralist, you must be content with a physiologist taking a " wide view of his subject."[1]

Mr. Spencer has a vision of the largeness of human nature, the great capabilities of the human soul

[1] Prolegomena to Ethics, p. 4.

Slowly and painfully he has wrought a system of what he calls ethical science, and it dooms the greatest gifts and powers of men to the pitiful uses of self-gratification; life becomes a miserable game. Is it too much to say that our scientific guides have been surprised and not a little dismayed at heart by the results of their own reasoning? It is as in the old story: the flask of natural science was opened to set free a genius who was to do everything for his discoverer, make him moral and happy, fill up all the gaps in his philosophy and experience. But the spirit once released has grown to awful proportions and now darkens over the trembling man whom it promised to serve. Evolution, that is, mechanical-causal development, reveals itself as a vast uncompromising necessity, and the moralist, prostrate on the ground, can only entreat the spirit to deal gently with its slaves. In the moment of dread suspense we hear him murmur to himself, "Can evolution be a mistake?" After all the effort and the reasoning he is back to that with a frightful urgency of doubt.

For this is now the point to which he is brought, that his question not only contains within it the seeds of scepticism but actually forces him into complete scepticism regarding the system of things of which he forms a part. If man's existence, man's progress in the past, his present beliefs and ideas are due to a single dominant process, what frightful insincerity, what horrible duplicity there must be somewhere in nature, since its creatures have learned to demand that which it cannot give and to seek a greatness for which there is no room. Above all, how comes it that the being whose place and destiny are of Nature's own appointing has always shrunk, and now as much as ever shrinks with bitterness or deep sadness, from her inexorable decree of death? Here is an abyss indeed unfathomable, unillumined.

Vainly does any one who believes in mere physical evolution try to separate man and his thought from the current of universal necessity, so that in him the fault may be found not in nature. The trick is ingenious, but is too trivial, too transparent, to answer the end. Consciousness is a disease, they say. But what, then, produced this disease? Nature? What right have we to speak of anything she does as disease? The word is one of our making, and if we were simple children of nature it would never have been coined. We should have suffered and died when our time came and never dreamed that anything else was possible. To find in our consciousness the faintest dislike of this or that which necessarily occurs to us is to have the whole nature philosophy thrown into sickening confusion. A law regulating all growth, vegetal and animal, covering the whole field of existence, without competition in the economy of the universe, could not so blunder as to produce creatures which impeached their destiny; nor could they whose lives are entirely in and of a certain system suspect the system to be anywhere at fault. Can we imagine the apples on a tree complaining that their fate is to ripen and fall to the ground? But they are not conscious. Well, what difference does consciousness make? Only this, that man, aware of his destiny, ought always to have glorified nature by intelligent acceptance of his fate.

So when Mr. Spencer asks the question, Is Evolution a mistake? he expresses the uttermost doubt of man, the scepticism of an evolutionist alone with the awful power he has confessed supreme, and knowing not how to win from it the demands of the human soul. What is tacit optimism? A foolish phrase covering despair. What is complete living and the happiness of the complete society? A dream within a dream, a fairy tale murmured in sleep to a crying child. What is the evolutionary ethic? A pretentious and laborious inanity.

At the last our philosopher stands revealed in his real character as the Æsculapius of the universe, and, we regret to add, very much of a quack. His great prescription is an ethical plaster which, if you only wear it long enough, you will get used to, and then you will not be able to do without it. The inventor stands in the market rehearsing the praises of his article, and the burden is this:—

"Not he who asserts that adaptations will increase is absurd,
But he who doubts that they will increase is absurd."

Well does our practitioner know that the thing can never cure either love or hate, sorrow or death. He knows that all the good of it is to make people think they are attending to their health when they are not. If the crowds flow past him to spend their substance on the gauds and sweetmeats of Vanity Fair, he has no right to claim their notice; he can give them nothing better than the trifles they are purchasing. His invention is a vanity like the rest, and though he vaunts the thing we defy him to believe in it.

For of what is it he needs to cure man if he is to have success as a healer? It is of nothing less than that insatiable desire inbred in him, deeply rooted in his being, for a something not yet realised. Along every line of his activity he is haunted by this craving which nature never satisfies; the attained ever whispers of an unattainable, the possessed of an unpossessed. Between him and the physical world the only equilibration is that death from which he instinctively recoils.

"In all your music one pathetic minor
  Your ears shall cross,
And all good gifts shall mind you of diviner
  With sense of loss."

And there is no remedy. For men, for societies, for the whole human race, one law holds in the vast dominion of force. The mightiest nation is but a wave in the weltering ocean which beats from cosmic shore to cosmic shore, unceasingly active, eternally impotent. What is it to a man that the wave of which he forms a part will have its flashing crest for a moment as it rolls in on some resounding beach? He is nothing; the ceaseless movement is all. Progress and momentary equilibrium become disintegration, the tide spends its rhythmic force upon one shore to rise upon another far off, again to surge in alternate advance and retreat

M

and beat towards a new point in the vastness of the Unmeasured. And ever there is darkness upon the rhythmic deep, darkness within it, a roar of energy, an awful heat of motion, but no eternal truth, no love that endures, no life that is not a movement towards death.

In this long story of cosmic change the truth for each man is that, in the physical scheme, he can gain and do up to a certain mark whether he make other people happy or not, that the "fire-spirits of dread desire" which are in him have but an hour in the night to work. To such an one it is vain to say, Evolution means this and foretells that: he will affirm, and with right, that Evolution for him is whatever he can accomplish or obtain. The preacher of social comfort will have nothing to say.

What is the author of the "Data of Ethics"? Is he a moralist, or an evolutionist, or a teacher of happiness culture? In vain he tries to act all the characters, and to combine their utterances in safe scientific formulæ. The thing cannot be done. The only result is a counterfeit gospel requiring a special education to read and a complete ignorance of Evolution to accept.

THE GOSPEL OF NATURE.

MATTHEW ARNOLD.

THE GOSPEL OF NATURE.

ATTEMPT after attempt has been made of late to extract from the ordinary course of things a rule for the guidance of mankind, a religion not altogether wanting in fervour, and having at least an air of wisdom and impressiveness. It is plain that the world cannot go on without something of the sort, for, however much we have outstripped our forefathers in mechanism and sanitation, we remain much like them in our need of comfort, stimulus, and hope. To some it is a vexation that life has mysteries which baffle the most acute research and troubles that will not be exorcised. But the heart of humanity still waits on mystery and expects a revelation of the meaning of sorrow and pain. Nor does the long habit of faith in an Unseen Ruler of the Universe give way to the arguments of atheism. Accordingly there are new Nature-Religions, echoing more or less the strain of ancient oracles, bearing like them burdens of woe and prophecies of coming good. The supernatural is banished, but something is retained to conjure with; the Universal Will, the Not-ourselves, the Service of Man are descanted on with a pathetic confidence that they are sufficient to keep alive the glow which dwelt in the old Faith and to exercise a power as great as any religion of miracle and prayer.

Now a notable thing in regard to the preachers of Nature-religion is the way in which they press Gospel phrases and ideas into their service, with the view of enlivening what would be otherwise a dull discourse. They appear to expect success only by imitating Christianity as far as possible, attiring their images in its robes and framing their sermons on the model of the orthodox, especially as regards the "dear brethren" and the "practical application." Nay, is not their spirit identical with that of Christianity? Are they not full of compassion for the multitudes who have been wandering about, misled by illusions and dreams?

There is no evident reason why Christians should be flattered by this sort of thing; but some of them are; and they show it in their wonderful deference to the arch-apostle of one of these new cults, the distinguished editor of our sacred books and expounder of the "method of Jesus." There seems to be an understanding among those who make any pretensions to acquaintance with the *Zeit-Geist* that Mr. Matthew Arnold has the destiny of religion in his hands. He is our Atropos—the wielder of the fatal shears; and many who cling to the old faith betray anxiety that he should deal gently with their creed. He sits as an oracle, and they bow their heads before the man who gibes at Shaftesbury and Ellicott and makes it his business to patronise Jesus Christ. For is he not gracious? While he denies their interpretations of the Bible, does he not praise the Bible itself ? While he has to excise the prophetical from the writings of the prophets, does he not urge us to study them? While he declares that miracles do not happen, does he not also declare that Jesus can never be superseded ? It is quite possible to endure sharp criticism of the Church and its bishops when sympathy so uncommon distinguishes the critic. May it not turn out that he is, after all, a builder, not a destroyer ? And then he has no desire to disestablish the Church. He has exposed the "narrowness and sterility" of dissent. Even denial of the supernatural served up in this manner is almost palatable, perhaps by-and-by will taste sweet when the appetite for it is acquired.

Shall we not say that the Laureate has prophesied of our ecclesiastical Merlin and this Vivien of criticism ?—Merlin suspicious, yet beguiled by treacherous caresses—

"He walked with dreams and darkness, and he found
A doom that ever poised itself to fall,
An ever-moaning battle in the mist,
World-war of dying flesh against the life,
Death in all life and lying in all love,
The meanest having power upon the highest,
And the high purpose broken by the worm.

．　　　．　　　．　　　．　　　．

And Vivien ever sought to work the charm
Upon the great Enchanter of the time,
As fancying that her glory would be great
According to his greatness whom she quenched."

How is it that those who have their place to vindicate as masters in Israel have not yet repelled Mr. Arnold's wily effort against Christianity? Has he cast the spell over them? Then, until they awake, the present discussion may at least show that there is no need to be at all alarmed by his strategy, however much it may offend.

Mr. Arnold should have "flourished" at the time of Christ, and been a Sadducee of high standing and influence in the Sanhedrin. Then of course he would have effected his mission. It would have been his, "taking God's Word under wise protection," to "correct its tendency to diffusiveness," to the legendary and "unverifiable," and by his clear reasoning to convince Christ that crucifixion would be a mistake, that Hellenism and its perfect lucidity afford the right method of establishing a religion. But he has come too late. The world has gone after the crucified Nazarene. Those who sit in the market-place will not mourn to the wailing nor dance to the piping of the belated prophet. Very likely he misunderstood the respect paid to him when he began to preach. He spoke so much of the Eternal, who "makes for righteousness," and of righteousness tending to life, that many fancied there must be at bottom a good deal in common between him and Christianity, and waited for it to appear. By this time, however, it is clear that his discovery is a mere formula, incomprehensible to those who have not learned the language in which it is written, worthless when comprehended.

Our teacher has undertaken to bring religion home to the most ordinary British stupidity; has staked his reputation, one seems to remember, on meeting the demand of the masses for plain saving truth. Surely, then, we are entitled to expect something that cannot fail to take hold of " uninstructed " persons—say the next couple one meets in the street—and compel them to own, some time or other, "a Power not themselves making for righteousness." But when we ask what the Eternal who loveth righteousness really is Mr. Arnold replies: "An imaginary recommendation of virtue, originated for practical purposes by—man himself, in a moment of religious genius." And when we further ask: "Is there, external to man or within him—in heaven, earth, or the abyss—an energy that may be trusted to raise him out of the miry clay?" the answer deliberately and definitely given is: "Yes; Nature;" and that is the last word.

Now this may be a gospel, and the darkness in which it leaves us, after all attempts to penetrate the cloud, may be that of imperfect eyes blinded by excess of light. After all, Mr. Arnold may be the true prophet he declares himself. Meanwhile, however, the vaunted clearness is very like that of the pane of glass in Dr. Hodgson's anecdote, a pane which took three persons to see through it.

Mr. Arnold's latest deliverance on the subject of religion is a "Comment on Christmas," which now appears along with "St. Paul and Protestantism."[1] He kept a certain Christmas Day by going to church, hearing the "roll" of some magnificent words of pro-

[1] Edition 1887.

phecy," joining in the Collect, and, on his return home, adding one or two more to his series of critical formulæ: "the multitude's high ideal of pureness," and "a necessary fact of nature." With the latter he proceeded to work cunningly, for the purpose of undermining the supernatural and establishing a religion of Nature in place of "popular Christianity." But he appears to have forgotten that Christmas Day, a "Discourse on Numbers," which he had already given in America. Taking these together, we shall inquire what his *Nature* really comes to.

The "Comment" begins by assailing an article of Christian faith which Mr. Arnold no doubt often reconnoitred before he hit upon a method of attack; and to this futile enterprise we may first give some consideration. He has a trick of fixing attention on certain adjuncts or circumstances of a doctrine, and, having easily blown them away, he then claims to have exploded the doctrine itself. Here, what he chooses to assail is the belief that Christ was born of a virgin; and he attacks it partly by criticism of a single Old Testament prophecy, partly by showing it to be legendary, and explaining how the legend arose.

As to the special prophecy on which he spends his criticism, it is a pity he wasted arrows upon it, for, as everybody knows, the belief of Christians in the Incarnation does not rest upon that. We maintain the doctrine to be interwoven with every personal claim Christ makes. We believe it to be the heart of the New Testament, the fulfilment of the hopes of mankind, the spring of all the life of the world's new age. It rests on facts which Mr. Arnold himself founds upon when he declares that Jesus is an *absolute*, that He stands above us all still, so that we cannot command Him. Our belief, therefore, would remain although Messianic prophecy disappeared in the fire of criticism; and there is no need to linger here with Mr. Arnold.

But the legend theory will delay us a little. We are told that the miraculous conception and birth of Jesus is "a lovely and attractive legend, which soon formed itself naturally and irresistibly around the origin of the Saviour."

A like story regarding Plato is brought forward; and it is affirmed that in either case the legend is a tribute to pureness. "In times and among minds where science is not a power, and where the preternatural is daily and familiarly admitted, the pureness and elevation of a great teacher strike powerfully the popular imagination, and the natural, simple, reverential explanation of His superiority is at once that He was born of a virgin."

As a rule Mr. Arnold is exceedingly careful. Has he shown his usual caution in this generalisation? Contemporary with Jesus, John Baptist, a teacher of rare pureness and elevation, appeared under circumstances favourable to the growth of such a legend. How is it that the story of his birth is altogether different? A little later, at the very time the legend is said to have arisen, we find another great teacher, remarkable for saintliness of life, whose name appears to have been exalted by some above that of Christ Himself. Did any such story ever connect itself with the Apostle Paul? How came it that, in a period "when the preternatural was daily and familiarly admitted," that "simple and reverential explanation" did not form around the origin of him who has been truly called "one of the great spirits of all time"? Pass to the twelfth century, when legends "grew on every tree." Of Dominic, the great popular teacher, whose miracles were superabundant, whose life was rigidly pure, stories innumerable are related to prove his extraordinary sanctity. Why is not this, that he was born of a virgin, one of them? Why was he called only the adopted son of Mary?

The parallel with Plato certainly remains. But Mr. Arnold knows quite well that about him there was another story, tracing his descent through Codrus to the god Poseidon. Is this explanation of his elevation and purity unnatural, as compared with the other? Or is that alone "natural and simple" which best serves the critic's purpose? In passing, one would like to know why the pureness of Plato is described as "signal and splendid," and his faith as "noble and serene," on the ground of the dry affirmation that "dissoluteness is to be condemned in that it brings about the aggrandisement of the lower side in our nature, and the defeat of the higher."

To proceed, however: "the legend of the Incarnation" is declared to be "the people's genuine translation of the fact of Christ's unique pureness." Chastity, it appears, was in the first century, "among the masses who love and foster legend," "a winning virtue." So the legend of the miraculous conception and birth of Christ is "the popular homage to a high ideal of pureness. It is the multitude's way of expressing for this its reverence." It is impossible not to pause here and ask what multitude Mr. Arnold is talking of. Is it among the masses of Corinth, Ephesus, Rome, Thessalonica, that we are to find this high ideal of pureness, and the popular homage to it?

The masses of our own time no doubt show a rough appreciation of this virtue; lewdness is unpopular, chastity is admired; but, even after Christianity has been at work for eighteen hundred years, is it possible to say more? Surely Mr. Arnold does not maintain that in this particular we have declined from the level of the first century! It is very easy to paint fancy pictures of that period; but since we are asked entirely to change our view of it, and that for the sake of a theory which is to abolish our faith in the Incarnation, we may fairly demand—On what facts, then? Where is the evidence on which you build?

In Rome, one would think, during the first century, pureness, not its opposite, was reckoned the burden. To select one fact: six vestals only were required; and the number was maintained with great difficulty, the most dreadful punishment failing to prevent their degradation. How could people who had breathed from infancy the polluted atmosphere of paganism at once estimate aright the purity of Christ, as far from coldness as it was from stain? The theory, be it observed, assumes that the popular mind was more impressed by the purity of Jesus than by any other manifestation of His nature. If this were true there would be evidence to prove it, but every fact points in another direction. The apostolic epistles afford the best information regarding the state of early Christian society. Do these epistles warrant the assumption of our theorist? Can any one read the letters of Paul to the Corinthians, Galatians, or Ephesians and not see how strenuously he was labouring to create in the minds of Christians the high ideal which we are asked to believe the masses were cherishing? In 1 Thess. iv. 6 is a remarkable expression: "The Lord is an avenger in all these things, as also we forewarned you and testified. . . . Therefore he that rejecteth" the gospel of pureness "rejecteth not man, but God." To the Ephesians, again, after speaking of the Gentiles, "who gave themselves up to work all uncleanness with greediness," he says: "But ye did not so learn Christ, *if so be that ye heard Him*"—one of his keen satirical touches, implying a doubt whether they had ever attended to the Master's teaching on this point. Was Paul ignorant of the time in which he lived? Was he a man to spend himself upon an unnecessary task?

But perhaps it was in Palestine that the "legend" arose. In society there we certainly see a favourable contrast to that of heathendom, and we find especially a high standard of purity maintained both by the

Pharisees and the Essenes. How does this bear on the theory of the legend? Taking the Essenes, it is plain that, since they were well known, their puritanism must have shaped the popular judgment regarding any one not a member of their sect. What evidence, then, is there that Jesus was distinguished, or could have been distinguished, for rigour of life, as compared with those ascetics? Was not His purity of so fine a quality that the masses failed to understand it?

One thing the people of Christ's time and after did believe in and venerate—His miraculous power. The evidence for this is overwhelming, and we should not have wondered if Mr. Arnold had made them explain that amazing power by saying that He was the Son of God, born in some miraculous way. But when the *pureness* of Christ is said to have struck the multitudes, it would surely have answered better to represent them as excusing their own laxity by making out Jesus utterly different from themselves. On this subject of purity there is a legend in Christendom, the development of which can be traced. But it has to do with the character of Christ's mother, not with His own. It is intended to explain, not how Mary could be the mother of a perfectly pure son, but how she could be "the mother of God." A thorough and fair examination of the belief as to the birth of our Lord will show it to be interwoven with faith in His Divine Sonship. The New Testament nowhere traces or suggests the connection which Mr. Arnold maintains; but it does continually ascribe the power and life of Christ to a unique superhuman origin; and the whole subtle enterprise against our faith in the Incarnation must fail ignominiously unless it can find better methods of attack. The author of the "Comment on Christmas" may claim to have invented an explanation of legend, itself wildly improbable, and a thousand times harder to receive than all the New Testament miracles put together. The reverence of the masses of the first century for purity, forsooth! Mr. Arnold required this ingredient in making his dynamite; and that is the only reason, so far as we can see, for the invention. But imagine the enterprise to have succeeded; imagine the method and secret of Arnold to have at last cleared all stupid *aberglaube* out of doors, leaving the house clean swept for the reign of "sweet reasonableness." The belief in a personal God is gone; the supernatural is gone; the Incarnation is brushed away. Well, the question now is: How without God to have religion; how without a Saviour to save man from his ruinous vices. Mr. Arnold may well say that virtue is in grave danger. Since he wrote, point has surely been given to that assertion. It is clear that he himself is impressed by a sense of possible, perhaps imminent catastrophe. Yea, verily, to save man is a necessity, and the attempt of the evangelist of lucidity is not less significant than his failure is instructive.

The watchword is Nature. "If pureness or any other virtue is still to subsist, it must subsist nowa-days, not by authority enforcing it in defiance of Nature, but because Nature herself turns out to be really for it." We must interpret Nature, and by Nature we must live. This, to borrow a phrase of Mr. Arnold's own, is a position which "requires great boldness and great lucidity;" and you would expect him next to tell us what the word *Nature* covers. Instead of doing so, however, he procures for himself very ingeniously a certificate that the position is all right and eminently sound. There is no need to be alarmed, for it is "the great Coleridgian position:" "Christianity, rightly understood, is identical with the highest philosophy, and, apart from all question of historical evidence, the essential doctrines of Christianity are necessary and eternal truths of reason— truths which man, by the vouchsafed light of Nature, and without aid from documents or tradition, may always and everywhere discover for himself."

Having quoted this very clear statement of Coleridge's principle, Mr. Arnold proceeds:—" When a Christian virtue is presented to us as obligatory, the first thing, therefore, to be asked is, whether our need of it is a fact of Nature."

Therefore—because this is the great Coleridgian position, and I have adopted it—a very adroit way of throwing dust in our eyes, so that we shall not see the moralist "fronting south by north"! Nevertheless, we have two or three questions to put to Mr. Arnold. Does he accept the phrase, "vouchsafed light of Nature," in the same sense as Coleridge? Does he maintain that any man's inductions from his own experience are necessary and eternal truths of reason?

Is the presentation of truth to man's reason the same as the enforcement of duty on man's conscience? And then, what right has Mr. Arnold to slip "facts of Nature" into the place of "necessary and eternal truths of reason," as if they meant precisely the same? "Christianity, rightly understood," says Coleridge, "is identical with the highest philosophy." Christianity, says Mr. Arnold, is lucidity, *plus* ancient rhetoric useful in kindling emotion. And Mr. Arnold claims to be at one with the great Coleridgian position!

But passing from this, we are speedily confronted with another question: If Nature is to "confirm or deny our instinctive anticipations," to "start us on our way," must it not be proved to speak in one clear tone and deliver one unwavering message? Popular Christianity does so; and Mr. Arnold must speak as definitely as popular Christianity if he is to effect anything. Does he? Let any reader refer to the serious admissions he has made as to the "mobility and variety in men's dispositions" which have often proved "fatal" to religion; or read his lines—

> "Nature with equal mind
> Sees all her sons at play;
> Sees man control the wind,
> The wind sweep man away;
> Allows the proudly riding and the foundered bark."[1]

These quotations might serve as mottoes for one portion at least of the "Comment on Christmas." For listen. "*Let us return to Nature* is a rising and spreading cry

[1] Empedocles on Etna.

now, as it was at the Renascence. And the Christian pureness has so much which seems to contradict Nature, and which is menaced by the growing desire and determination to return to Nature. The virtue has suffered more than most virtues in the hands of hypocrites; and with hypocrites and hypocrisy as a power in human life, there is an increasing impatience. But the virtue has been mishandled also by the sincere, but who are at the same time over-rigid, formal, sour, narrow-minded; and these, too, are by no means in the ascendant among us just now." This does not refer to the asceticism of the Church of Rome, for he speaks separately of that. It means unmistakably that people may be too chaste, and that Nature does not demand the severity of puritanism. We have heard this sort of thing often enough; but we certainly did not expect to hear it from Mr. Arnold, especially as he professes to sympathise with the "sacrificed classes." As for the declaration that the decline of hypocrisy and the decline of sincerity are both helping the cause of pureness, that may seem at first sight mysterious, not to say absurd; but only to persons who do not understand logic. The argument is plain. Nature is for purity. Hypocrisy and narrow-minded sincerity damage purity. They must both, therefore, be unnatural, and it is only their decline that can assist the growth of pureness. If the Illogical still objects that hypocrisy and sincerity are "facts of Nature," and therefore ought to help virtue by their growth instead of their decline, we refer him to Mr. Arnold. He wrote the "Comment on Christmas."

But the new gospel proceeds to acknowledge "a growing sense that gaiety and pleasure are *legitimate demands of our nature*," and that with this growing sense comes the multiplication everywhere of the means of gaiety and pleasure, all which " solicits the senses, makes them bold, eager, and stirring." At the same time, " the force of old sanctions of self-restraint diminishes and gives way." And so we are led to the conclusion, already quoted, that "if pureness or any other virtue is still to subsist," it must be, not by authority of the old theological kind enforcing it, but " because nature herself turns out to be really for it." The pane of glass seems to be thickening. It will take a dozen robust, non-lucid British Philistines to see through it soon. For if the love of pleasure is not natural to man, how does he experience it? And if the gratification of bodily appetites is natural, how can it ever be impure? And if it is often impure, so that a moral law is needed, then what about "Nature"?

There is a cry that we return to Nature, and that cry menaces pureness. Men of the Renascence took the way their nature inclined, and it was not that of pureness. Men of Corinth and Rome in the first century did the same, as men of Athens had done before them, and went far from pureness; yet in that very century the masses reverenced purity so much that they cherished a legend in its honour, so bringing to light a necessary fact of Nature. Thus men who were so far from the truth of things as to believe, if not invent, an incredible legend were yet able to perceive and value necessary facts of Nature, now lost sight of in our growing desire to return to Nature. What sort of stuff is this? And what does Mr. Arnold mean by it? He seems to be equally divided between the views of Nature propounded by Mr. Snawley and Mr. Squeers in a certain memorable dialogue,[1] and to be writing a commentary which shall satisfy both parties. It is an unworthy enterprise, and the writer must be told plainly that on a point so momentous we have a right to claim the utmost "vigour and rigour" both in logic and in morals.

Evolutionary theories of the origin of man make short work of this "necessary fact of Nature"—that it is for pureness; and one who occupies Mr. Arnold's position can scarcely leave them out of account. A critic of the Darwinian school, if he cared to mention anything so obvious, would remind our author that polygamy has been practised since the dawn of history by races civilised and uncivilised; and a disrespectful critic might ask whether Mr. Arnold had this in his mind when he spoke of the over-rigid and sour, and whether we may expect to hear by-and-by of the lucidity, freedom, and breadth of Salt Lake society.

Is there any way of escape from this tangle? Yes.

---

[1] *Nicholas Nickleby*, ch. xlv. : " ' It only shows what natur' is, sir,' said Mr. Squeers. 'She's a rum un, is natur'.' 'She is a holy thing, sir,' remarked Snawley. 'I believe you,' added Mr. Squeers, with a moral sigh. 'I should like to know how we should ever get on without her. Natur',' said Mr. Squeers solemnly, 'is more easier conceived than described. Oh what a blessed thing, sir, to be in a state of natur'!'"

"His own experience may in the end be the surest teacher for every man; but meanwhile . . . testimony as to the experience of others, general experience, is of the most serious weight and value." Certainly; then let us have it. *Sine vita non vivitur;* show us lives which prove the necessity of virtue, which establish beyond all question the natural worth and obligation of pureness.

Well, we have borne a good deal so far, knowing that our friend had a theory to prove, and must be humoured; but when he names his witnesses, the time to revolt has come, for one of them is Goethe, and another is—Ninon de l'Enclos! Goethe, whose certificate will not be of much account to those who can justify themselves by appealing to his practice; and Ninon, one of the most notorious of courtesans.

To be sure, there are two other certificates—one from Sophocles, and one from Madame de Sévigné; but as Goethe is ranked with Sophocles and Plato among the "loftiest spirits of this world," and Ninon de l'Enclos with Madame de Sévigné among the most lucid, and the one testimony seems every bit as useful as the other, we are driven to ask—Is purity after all of much consequence? Human nature being the court of appeal, men and women are brought forward, chosen out of all time, to give evidence. But they are not chosen for their purity, their saintliness. Take even Madame de Sévigné, whose life was regular enough. Are we to be instructed in virtue by a woman who laughed at the sufferings of the Huguenots and applauded the revocation of the Edict of Nantes? After all the talk about pureness and "grave danger," it "turns out" that lucidity is the main thing, the saving salt—so far as there is any saving at all. "If ye were blind," said the Master, upon whom Mr. Arnold is to improve, "ye should have no sin: but now ye say, We see; therefore your sin remaineth."

The question being of human nature, the witnesses chosen must of course have something to tell. But our instructor has himself taught us to consider *conduct;* to look there, and there only, for the real nature and belief of a man. The religion of Israel was entirely concerned with conduct, we were told, and the teaching of Jesus is in the same line. It is, accordingly, the conduct of Mr. Arnold's witnesses with which we are concerned. Their lucidity we may admit, since it is pressed upon our attention; but on a moral question we distinctly refuse to take a few casual remarks as the sum of evidence. If Nature spoke through these persons, it was not when they posed themselves to deliver fine sentiments, but when they went freely about the business of living. We adapt Mr. Arnold, as he has adapted Dr. Johnson, and commend the word to all whom it may concern: "Fine sentiments about purity are the last refuge of a scoundrel."[1] They are the homage of loose persons to outraged morality.

The prophets prophesy to Ninon of "eternal purity." Does she believe them? Perhaps, when she has sucked

[1] Discourses in America, p. 52.

her orange and finds the rind bitter. When the orange lay in her hand she did not think pureness on the whole the most useful. And with Nature alone for a guide, why should she? "Nature," she might have said, "has given me beauty and wit, and for these, as the world goes, I can have luxury, flattery, variety, the admiration of great men. I like these things, and why may I not have them?" So when she sold herself, what Arnold would ever have persuaded her to a different course? "Nature is for purity," says the moralist. "May be," says Ninon, with a laugh; "some kinds of nature. That is the appropriate utterance of a jaded mind.[1] I acknowledge nothing that may misdirect or retard me in the effort towards a complete, many-sided existence or curtail my natural liberty of heart and mind." So she too can use the word *Nature* skilfully; and what is there to say? Something the moralist murmurs about "living in the eternal order that never dies." "But what," she asks, being a very practical person, "will you promise me if I take your way? I shall prove my lucidity? I shall belong to your order? Oh, thank you!—but regularity is a dull and stupid business; you may have a turn for it; I have not; I like pleasure." And when at the end she says, "If I had known, I would rather have hanged myself," her own world will just observe that this also is the appropriate utterance of a jaded mind—a mere pathological symptom. As for our moralist, he can but lament the irremediable. Ninon was equal to

[1] We borrow here a phrase or two from "Marius, the Epicurean."

making a bad bargain with the world; that was all. Yes; lucidity can be trusted so far as this: having failed to keep us pure during a whole life, to wake up at the end and damn us. A gospel here!—say rather a torch flashing over the gulf of despair.

Mr. Huxley is reported to have once said: "The man of science who commits himself to even one statement which turns out to be devoid of good foundation loses somewhat of his reputation among his fellows; and if he is guilty of the same error often, he loses not only his intellectual but his moral standing, for it is justly felt that errors of this kind have their root rather in the moral than the intellectual nature." This ruling is just; and we leave it with the remark that in dealing with moral questions and the nature of man a moral use of testimony is supremely necessary; we expect to find no garbling of evidence, no *hocus pocus*.

A prophet who at one time prays us to remember that "the brilliant Greece perished for lack of attention enough to conduct;" that its successor, the Renascence, an Ishmael, a "brilliant new-comer, with his animating maxim, *Let us return to Nature*, . . . died of provoking a collision with the homely Isaac, righteousness:" that France, developing *l'homme sensuel moyen* "without misgivings," attracts everybody, has " success," but has also repeated " disasters,"[1]—a prophet, we say, who at one time, with a deep moral sigh, prays us to remember all this, and a while afterwards declares to us that Nature is the mother and nurse of virtue,

[1] Literature and Dogma, second edition, pp. 354-356.

which can live only as it draws nutriment from her breast—is certainly not the free, lucid person he would have us believe, and is no way entitled to accuse Protestantism of "rude and blind criticism." But even if his criticism were very much "alive at an unusual number of points"—man cannot live by criticism alone. What motive does he give us? As a moralist, he should be able to show the "risk" and define the "peril" of which he speaks. And when, instead of doing that, he busies himself in making neat phrases to convince lucid friends and puritan opponents that on the moral question he is "right," we know what will come of it. As Deutsch used to say when any one disappointed him: "Go down! go down!" The puritan preacher does not so fail in his practical application.

> "Deliver not the tasks of might
> To weakness."

Nature, one would think, is powerful enough to achieve her ends. Mr. Arnold has spoken of "hitting the mark." That, it may be said, Nature always does. Whatever is her business she does magnificently, at any cost, in spite of all our groans and curses. She overloads our instincts, as Emerson says, that she may be sure of us. "Wary Nature makes us a little wrong-headed in that direction in which we are rightest, and on goes the game again with new whirl for a generation or two more." For unreckoned centuries Nature has toiled at her Titanic enterprise, and her breath does not fail; her hand is still firm and keen; victoriously she goes on her way, and will go on hitting the mark for another millennium or two. Why not leave Nature to her work? Does she not confront us with her cool air and say : " So hot, my little men! Be sure I can manage my own business."

Ah! Mr. Arnold replies, you are perverting my meaning altogether; this is really very crude and blind criticism. Have I not told you that 'impulses proceed from two sources, quite different, and of quite different degrees of authority;'[1] that morality is changed to religion when we grasp the idea of *two lives*, — one of them the higher self, 'life properly so called;' the other 'a lower transient self,' which is 'the following of the wishes of the flesh and of the current thoughts'? Have I not begged the world to remember that 'the free development of our *apparent* self has to undergo a profound modification from the law of our higher, *real* self—the law of righteousness?' The Nature I speak of, when I enforce morality, is not 'the present constitution of things,' but the issue of things; . . . 'conscience and the issue of things go together.'[2]

You split "Nature" in two, then, making one part work contrary to the other? But by what right? Nature is one ; Nature is impartial. You ascribe great authority to one " self," while you keep the other in subjection ; on what ground do you make that fantastical division ? Suppose that under some circumstances Nature develops the idea of purity, and even produces a race of men who are convinced that purity is essential, she must do this in just the same

[1] Literature and Dogma, p. 201 *et seq.*   [2] Ibid., p. 350.

way as she produces strength and the belief that strength is best. Where do you find the emphasis on purity necessary to establish the ideal? Speaking generally, Nature is against dissoluteness as it is against dishonesty,—that is, experience shows a certain amount of order to be necessary for society, and so you get the emphasis which makes the law. Civil society, emerging from chaos, creates a rule sufficient for its purposes. Beyond this Nature alone cannot go. And Mr. Arnold, having himself insisted that we must "use words as mankind generally use them," cannot employ "Nature" to cover something else. For the ideal of pureness, as for any other ideal, Nature makes no provision. Just as she is, in the main, for self-preservation, not disinterestedness, so she is in the main for perpetuating the race and for the maintenance of families, but not for absolute purity. To Nature the pure man, finding his happiness in purity, is no more than the strong man rejoicing in his strength. They are both her children, as are the oak and the lily.

> "She cries : ' A thousand types are gone :
> I care for nothing, all shall go.
> Thou makest thine appeal to me :
> I bring to life, I bring to death !'"

Mr. Arnold may well say, "Ah, what pitfalls are in that word *Nature!*"

One of Mr. Arnold's authorities is Goethe. He, while desiring to conserve all which, as he said, "culture has won of Nature," avowed marriage to be "unnatural,"—that is, Nature cannot furnish or sustain the ideal of purity. Her aims forbid disorder, inordinate concupiscence, but they do not forbid such freedom and easiness as Goethe allowed himself; they do not forbid a George Sand, a Burns. If they did, a George Sand, a Burns could not exist.

But we depend on conscience and the issue of things, which "go together." Here is fine reasoning! What is this but the "unverifiable," so often and scornfully repudiated? How is conscience, as a product of Nature, to assert a principle which the operations of Nature have not yet demonstrated? If Nature is prognosticating an issue, science ought to be clearly indicating that issue. At least our best observers ought to be aware of it, foreseeing it. Huxley and Tyndall should be eloquent expounders of it; it should be finding a place in our manuals and popular lectures. Is it so? If it were, Mr. Arnold's edition of the Bible would be a superfluity. Astronomy and geology have something to say about the destiny of this world, but they do not require the Bible to back them up. Mr. Arnold, enunciating a new law of Nature, for which he has not yet found a name, needs not trouble himself about the Bible any more than the astronomer does. Why should he beat the bush with such labour, such deep emotion, in order to start the hare? If Nature has that matter in hand she will duly effect it.

But we have not yet done with Mr. Arnold's Nature. As individuals have a best and real self, so have races and nations. Salvation for them depends upon the bulk and power of the "remnant." "The majority are bad," said one of the wise men of Greece; but he was a pagan. Much to the same effect, however, is the famous sentence of the New Testament, " Many are called, few chosen." " This appears a hard saying, . . . but turn it how you will, the few, as Cardinal Newman well says, can never mean the many. . . . Perhaps you will say that the majority is sometimes good; that its impulses are good generally, and its action is good occasionally. Yes, but it lacks principle, it lacks persistence; if to-day its good impulses prevail, they succumb to-morrow; sometimes it goes right, but is very apt to go wrong. . . . The world being what it is, we must surely expect the aims and doings of the majority of men to be at present very faulty."[1] Except for the conventional exegesis of a famous and perpetually misread text, this might pass. Mr. Arnold goes on for some time proving from Plato and Isaiah that "the majority is always unsound," that the only hope lies in what he calls the "comfortable doctrine of the remnant." Nature is now discovered to be in the majority "very faulty;" and even the remnant does not always save. "It always bears a small proportion to the majority," and "the grave thing for states like Judah and Athens is that the remnant is, must, in positive bulk be so small, and therefore so powerless for reform." Passing next to speak of the difference in races, he shows us how, as German seriousness dies out of the Gaul, it leaves the average sensual man, who is "ludicrously insufficient on the moral side," taking

[1] Discourses in America, p. 6 et seq.

"fine sentiments" for "serious moral ideas." The Gallic nature, he tells us, is for sensuality and gaiety; the Teutonic for steadiness and seriousness; and M. Renan can actually say that "Nature cares nothing about chastity." So it comes to this, that some races have, properly speaking, no inclination for purity; that the majority always and everywhere is unsound, and that even our Teutonic nature, which "cares about chastity a good deal," is decent only because we have a large remnant.

Here, then, we have a distinct admission that evolution has never produced a sound community and cannot ensure the "issue of things" which conscience foretells. It is quite a chance, so to speak, if Nature maintains purity at all. And if at last we inquire how then she is to do what the "Comment on Christmas" demands of her in the way of establishing Christian pureness, we discover that nothing of the sort is looked for. The whole dependence "turns out" finally to be upon Germanic seriousness and that discredited "authority" which, thrust aside at the outset as utterly effete, is now in effect recalled and placed in command. "As a stage and a discipline, and as means for enabling that poor, inattentive, and immoral creature man (!) to love and appropriate and make part of his being divine ideas, on which he could not otherwise have laid or kept hold, the discipline of Puritanism has been invaluable; and the more I read history, the more I see of mankind, the more I recognise its value."[1] So far in the "Discourse on

[1] Discourses in America, p. 70.

Numbers;" and in the "Comment on Christmas" we find a panegyric of Christ equally significant: Christ is an *absolute*; "we cannot get behind Him and above Him, cannot command Him. But even were Jesus less of an *absolute* than He is, . . . still the personage of Jesus and the Christian rules of conduct and recommendations of virtue . . . would have a value which no new apparitions and constructions can possibly have. . . . The way, truth, and life have been found in Christianity, and will not now be found outside of it."

Now in our reading of it this means that Christianity and Puritanism are forces of the Over-nature; efficacious, therefore, where Nature ceases; and that Mr. Arnold, constrained to abjure the vain pedantries of Positivism —although that system is his natural resting-place— is under the necessity of returning to divine religion in order to find any hope for the future of the world. But in Mr. Arnold's private interpretation what does it mean? Simply that in Puritanism we have a current of the vague stream of tendency making for righteousness, somewhat turbid and vehement for cultured taste, still the most living water which has yet flowed from the rock of Nature; and that in Christ we have the supreme example of lucidity—except, perhaps, Mr. Arnold himself. It is very kind of him to say that Christ is an *absolute*, and to give Christianity new certificates; very good of him to encourage his Anglican friends in saying their Collects and observing Christmas, Easter, nay, even Trinity Sunday. If he goes on like this a while longer we shall see him in the churchyard some day, picking up and tenderly dusting the Athanasian Creed. But when he commends Christianity as useful because it yields surface springs of emotion which, until they run dry, the clergy may "beneficially" turn to account, we take leave to tell him that, in the guise of a simple-minded man, with a single eye to the glory of God, he is vainly attempting to "play tricks with our understanding." For the rest of the term of this world people are to be making-believe very hard and to call it progress. We, for our part, are deeply concerned, not merely with the good behaviour of the masses, but with the salvation of society; not merely to keep the East End quiet and —"sacrificed,"[1] by means of an old charm and a cloudy sketch of judgment, but here and now to redeem the "sacrificed" and the "idolaters" alike, so that, as brothers, they may share and help forward the "renovation."

What use can Mr. Arnold make of his doctrine of Nature when he is brought face to face with the miseries and cravings of a great city, where the problems of human life crowd as thickly as the people? A few weeks before the "Comment" was written its author was summoned to the east end of London, to give the "sacrificed classes" what help and direction he could. We mean no disrespect to those who invited him when we say that he set out, like a modern Balaam, to condemn the people who trust to a supernatural guide

[1] See *Daily News*, December 1, 1884.

and helper, who expect shortly to enter a land of promise. And he improved upon Balaam; he was even more Sphinx-like than the original. He allowed the "charm" of a new heaven and a new earth; nay, he went so far as to assert that some day a renovation will come. There is comfort in the idea, and people who live in Bethnal Green or Whitechapel need moral opium of one kind or another. Surveying this poor blind Israel, with its crude visions, he really pities it; feels inspired to utter a few kindly warnings, a few vague consolations; at the same time never forgetting that a certain cultured Balak stands a little way off, wondering what this prophet, whom he is able to promote to great honour, means; what he thinks he can effect. He knows quite well, however, what he is doing; he knows that it takes a great deal of lucidity to sit quietly starving in the East End after the West End has abolished God and the future life. "There is no Divine Father; no immortality except the ideal society of the future, which none of us will ever see; no clearing up of the problems of righteousness arising in each life; no vindication of pain, sorrow, poverty, death? Why, then, let us help ourselves wherever we can; let us force our way into Canaan at once, by all possible means. If there is nothing but this life, we must *have* it. The good Lord Jesus has had His day. Do not talk about the judgment of the prince of this world; let us see it done; let us do it ourselves. If we are to be any the better for it, the affair must not be delayed."

Balaam understands the danger, and, to Balak's astonishment, he neither curses at all nor blesses at all. Let them give diligent attendance at Bethnal Green Museum. Study of water-colour drawings and Chinese pottery may do wonders for them. Frequent contemplation of grinning Japanese figures may elevate their spirits above the cares and worries of life. And for Balak, let him be warned in time. "Said I not unto thee, What the Lord saith that will I speak?"

A "*not us* making for righteousness," abstract, impersonal—what is this for practical purposes? Men will mind such a stream of tendency as little as we here mind the Amazon or the Orinoco. It brings to bear on us no pressure of responsibility; yet without responsibility and the gravity it gives to life you will have—not *men* at all—only bubbles, feathers blown about with every wind; no materials for society; nothing but flimsy units, incoherent because imponderable. We talk of what men may do, what culture may do for them, what it is well for them to avoid, well for them to follow. But *may* and *should* will never save. It is necessary to tell men what they *must* do; what, by laws they cannot evade, they are bound to do. This is the only effectual principle of human progress. By some teachers of religion it is not properly recognised. They attempt, it has been well said, to save men as if they were invalids, by providing hospitals and convalescent homes for them, or as if they were victims of enchantment, by uttering over them a formula which breaks the spell and sets them free. And so these teachers achieve little in proportion to their zeal and apparent success. Salvation is not a miraculous *tour de force* apart from the laws of our life and proper humanity.

Now, responsibility to self or self-made law is nothing. No society has ever attempted to exist on the basis that every man should do what is right in his own eyes; and degrees of culture make no difference here. Individualism in morals is altogether an absurdity. Nor is responsibility to fellow-men, apart from any further reference, of much account,—a mere matter of police. Neither any man nor any association of men has the right to lord it over me. Let who will object to my proceedings, I may just as properly object to theirs. Although they compel me to submit to their way, they show no real authority over me. I shall not acknowledge a duty because a thousand or ten thousand insist upon it—else all the errors men have ever cherished would impose themselves upon me. It is notorious that half the business of life consists in sifting human theories, in rejecting or modifying what humanity urges. The *spectres of the tribe* can never furnish a law of life to thoughtful men, who must, nevertheless, have a law of life and march in rank with their fellows. As for those we call immoral, dishonest, cruel, it would be a question whether we have any right to brand them with such names. If thieves should claim the liberty to measure their wits against our precautions, we could not logically deny their claim; we could only double the number of police. Why may not the thief condemn society, as well as society condemn the thief? To this it must come if the ground of duty goes no deeper than the vote of the greater number. The whole question is of ability, cunning. Each takes as much of his own way as every other man's way will allow. There is no more responsibility than among the animals in a forest—elephant and snake, tiger and fawn, humming-bird, nightingale, cockatoo and leaf-insect; each is good after its kind and follows the instincts of its race. Then, according to science, the fittest will survive. This is nature. With a theory of responsibility which rests on the authority of the "better self" or the "remnant" you can reach no higher. Between social order and chaos there is but an accidental separation, varying, indefinite. Yet on this we are asked to rely. "If there were no moral law it would be necessary to invent one." The trouble is to invent one that will not founder ignominiously on its trial trip, as the new religions of the nineteenth century are apt to do.

We want responsibility still, so that we may have men and the makings of society. Let us question popular Christianity; and we shall not allow ourselves to be troubled about aberrations or unverifiable garniture. We have to do with essentials. To begin, Christianity, as universally believed, lays down a clear and adequate law of obligation, intelligible to everybody, finding support in the human conscience everywhere. It declares that each man, as existing—with his own sphere of energy, his personal identity and a measure of freedom—stands related intimately, directly to the source of existence, the fountain and limit of personal freedom. It emphatically contradicts the notion that any man can be a law to himself, and the other notion that in moral affairs a majority may rule. It enforces obligation by revealing to men, beyond Nature, a kingdom of which they are all subjects, sustaining relations to one another and to its eternal laws. It addresses even to the most ignorant, the most degraded, a solemn call to be a man and act a man's part: "Arise, and stand upon thy feet. Thou art of value in the universe; thou hast a place to fill, a destiny to accomplish." At the same time to the Sévignés and Goethes, standing apart in a region of culture and self-enjoyment, it carries the needful message: "What have you been? What have you done? There is One to whom you also must render account."

Here Christianity begins; and having brought home responsibility to man and stirred him to think of duty, it proceeds without delay to meet his reasonable claim, his persistent desire for a correlative right or hope; so that duty is not left a cruel burden impossible to bear, or even to admit in thought. Modern altruism, strangely, sadly inexorable, forces upon man a weight of care and stoically forbids him to indulge a single personal expectation; it is a new and subtler asceticism, without the vision that made bright the desert hermitage. Not so Christianity. While it says emphatically, This must be done, This law is imperative,

THE GOSPEL OF NATURE.

eternal, it points to the origin of law in the character of a Divine Father, infinitely generous and patient, who is on the side of the human race; His commands are imperative, because they are benignant; uncompromising, because they are supremely wise; His will and purpose for man have been unfolding themselves in history, enforcing themselves in providence from age to age, with a marvellous blending of severity and gentleness, the expression of a serious far-reaching love; so the Christian idea of responsibility creates a grave, resolute type of character, because it rests on the eternal power and certain judgment of God; and its complement is the idea of redemption, charged with strength, joy, promise for every human being, however low in the scale, opening to the heavy laden a door of boundless hope.

So, along with the responsibility of man to his Maker, comes another responsibility, that assumed by Christ,—the grace of God that bringeth salvation; and Redemption utters itself, becomes the keynote of the march of life. Here is love demanding and answering to love. Here is sacrifice requiring and answering to sacrifice. In Jesus Christ the Divine light of compassion and righteousness burns into a focus, the clear radiance of which illuminates the dark regions of human experience. What is Mr. Arnold's Christ? An accident; a unique and fortunate accident of human development? An *absolute?* But why? How can Mr. Arnold, on his own premises, be so sure that Christ is an *absolute?* Why not Plato? Why not himself?

There are a good many people who will avow that Jesus of Nazareth is too pure, too spiritual for this world; that *necrosis* is an "aberration of theological dogma." The supremacy of Jesus, what is it? That of One who confidently offers to our race what no other acknowledged leader ever thought of offering in his own name, his own power. And yet He, in whom we reverence a majestic type never realised elsewhere, of truth, dignity, and holiness, is not self-centred, but testifies of His relation to a Father who sent Him, a Father to whom we also are related, with whom we must come to be one, as He is. He sweetens responsibility to us by undertaking duties like ours, a burden like that we have to bear; and His life and death bring redemption by lifting us out of sin and weakness into His own freedom and exaltation, His own life of obedience and love, which is eternal.

It is easy to understand why Mr. Arnold has had to drop lucidity and Nature after all his attempts to conjure with them, and has turned wistfully to Christ. So must all systems of thought, all schemes of renovation. Without this life there is no living; without this energy there is no going forward to the heights of being that await us. "The preaching of Jesus Christ" is "the revelation of the mystery which hath been kept in silence through times eternal, but now is manifested, and, according to the commandment of the eternal God, is made known unto all nations unto obedience of faith." Yes; Mr. Arnold may well look wistfully to Christ; he may well cast backward glances at the old Puritanism, and call it "that excellent discipline." For, whatever dissent there may be from this doctrine or that method, there is no denying that Puritanism has given the world men of massive build, moral giants who have won the great battles of freedom and pushed forward the outposts of the advancing race. And their strength lay in their belief. A righteous God, to whose will man is reconciled by the life and death of Christ; a narrow way of faith and discipline for each human being; a Divine judgment, and an immortal soul;—from these conceptions, as from a mighty root, has grown all that is strong, free, and fruitful in Western civilisation. We challenge culture and naturalism to show in any of their disciples a tithe of the vigour with which "popular Christianity" has inspired thousands and tens of thousands. Attic salt, delightful as it is in the flavouring of life, is not food-stuff; man lives as he is resolute, sincere, unfaltering in truth and purity; and that which enables struggling men and women to live such a life can only be a force of the Over-natural, the Spiritual, the Divine.

THE END.

RECENT WORKS

ON

CHRISTIAN EVIDENCES AND APOLOGETICS.

GOSPELS OF YESTERDAY: DRUMMOND—SPENCER—ARNOLD.
By ROBERT A. WATSON, M.A. Second Edition. Crown 8vo, 5s.

"The attempt to refute these three influential and very different writers in one small volume is a bold one, but we must declare it successful. . . . By 'Gospels of Yesterday' Mr. Watson probably means Gospels that till yesterday were unheard of. He has done much to make his title true in another sense, namely, that whatever claim these Gospels had set up to be listened to yesterday, the ground is cut from under them to-day."—*Church Bells.*

"The many attractive features of Professor Drummond's book, and its great popularity and influence, make it all the more necessary for those who dissent from its teaching to state their reasons for dissent. Mr. Watson has done this part of his work with great incisiveness and power. So thorough is the criticism, so powerfully does he set forth the inconsistencies of the writing under his notice, that we are inclined to feel sympathy with the author, and to ask whether he has not misinterpreted the meaning of Professor Drummond. But no: he gives chapter and verse, and each proposition he combats is fully given. . . . If Mr. Watson had nothing more in this book than his criticism of Mr. Spencer, he would have done most effective service. . . . We should like much if this part (that dealing with Mr. Spencer's 'Data of Ethics') of Mr. Watson's book could be put into the hands of many."—*British Weekly.*

ST. JOHN THE AUTHOR OF THE FOURTH GOSPEL. By HOWARD HEBER EVANS., B.A., Author of "St. Paul the Author of the Acts of the Apostles and the Third Gospel." Extra crown 8vo, 6s.

"While this treatise will be sufficient for the ordinary reader, it will help the student of theology to sources of information which otherwise he might overlook."—*Church Bells.*

BY THE SAME AUTHOR.

ST. PAUL THE AUTHOR OF THE LAST TWELVE VERSES OF THE SECOND GOSPEL. Crown 8vo, 2s. 6d.

THE NATURAL ELEMENTS OF REVEALED THEOLOGY.
By the Rev. GEORGE MATHESON, D.D. Crown 8vo, 6s.

"It would be hard to find any small volume in which the immense need for the Christian Revelation, and the Divine, all-satisfying character of that Revelation are more lucidly and attractively set forth."—*Expositor.*

ALIKE AND PERFECT; or, God's Three Revelations. By the Rev. C. A. WILLIAMS. Crown 8vo, 3s. 6d.

"The idea of the book is familiar, but the treatment has all the freshness, crispness of speech, fertility of illustration, and directness of purpose that characterise much of the best American literature. In harmonising God's revelation of Himself in the spheres of Creation, Providence, and the Divine Word, the author avoids much of the argumentation we are accustomed to on this theme, and leads us into tracts of thought at once suggestive and impressive."—*Presbyterian Magazine.*

"This valuable treatise will prove attractive alike in its descriptions of natural scenery, in its references to the finger of God in history, and in its clear enunciation of the Divine method for fallen man's restoration."—*Record.*

THE BIBLE TRUE TO ITSELF: A Treatise on the Historical Truth of the Old Testament. By the Rev. A. MOODY STUART, D.D. New Edition. Crown 8vo, 5s.

"The argument is elaborate, both in plan and execution. The four principal topics are Deuteronomy, the Mosaic authorship of the Pentateuch, the order of the Old Testament development, and the unity of Isaiah. The orderly, cumulative character of the argument may be gathered from the treatment of the second point. The volume is a profitable one both for head and heart."—*London Quarterly Review.*

"The untenableness of much modern criticism is shown in a few chapters, which must make the book a standard one. On other points raised by the destructive school, the reasoning is calm, candid, and convincing."—*Christian.*

BY THE SAME AUTHOR.

ISRAEL'S LAWGIVER: His Narrative True and His Laws Genuine. Crown 8vo, 2s. 6d.

"We have to express our thankful admiration of the way in which Dr. Moody Stuart has accomplished his task, and our hope that his scholarly dissertation may receive the calm consideration of those whose minds may have been disturbed and convictions shaken by recent critical speculations."—*Messenger (Presbyterian).*

ROCK VERSUS SAND; or, The Foundations of the Christian Faith. By J. MONRO GIBSON, D.D. Small crown 8vo, 1s. 6d.

"Dr. Gibson, adapting the architectonic symbolism of a house, discourses on the foundation and structure of Christian character and life. The Foundation is God; the Chief Corner Stone, God in Christ; the Foundation of the Apostles and Prophets, God in Christ made known by the Prophets. It is an Apologia for Christianity, and deals with the popular infidel objections of the day. Dr. Gibson is an acute observer and a cogent reasoner. His little book is strong and timely."—*British Quarterly Review.*

"This volume displays rare skill and originality in its structure and composition. We commend the book most heartily, as one in every way serviceable to the cause of truth. The style is popular, without being loose; the arguments full, without being diffuse; and the criticism of opponents firm and bold, without being harsh or one-sided."—*Christian.*

CHRISTIANITY, SCIENCE, AND INFIDELITY: A Vindication of the Received Truths of our Common Faith. Showing the Follies and Absurdities of Atheism. By the Rev. WILLIAM HILLIER, Mus. Doc. Second Edition. Crown 8vo, 2s.

"The volume gives, in orderly and clear outline, some history of the origin and influence of Christianity, with an elaborate exposition of the argument from design, and the testimony of science. Mr. Hillier's treatment of his important subject is lucid and careful, and his book should be of help in forming opinion."—*Literary World.*

THE PERSON OF CHRIST: The Perfection of His Humanity Viewed as a Proof of His Divinity. By PHILIP SCHAFF, D.D. Crown 8vo, 3s. 6d.

NISBET'S THEOLOGICAL LIBRARY.

Extra Crown 8vo.

CHRISTIANITY ACCORDING TO CHRIST. By the Rev. J. MONRO GIBSON, D.D. 6s.

"Almost every sentence in this book is plain and sensible, and full of judicious useful teaching. The careful reader, seeking for the truths which are really original, for the first simplicity of the Gospel, will find much to reward his study."—*Scots Observer.*

"Dr. Gibson is a master in reasoning, and solidly supports his main thesis. We warmly commend the work as equally fitted to help the doubter and to edify the believer."—*Christian.*

THE GOSPEL ACCORDING TO ST. PAUL: Studies in the First Eight Chapters of the Epistle to the Romans. By the Rev. J. OSWALD DYKES, D.D. 6s.

"Dr. Dykes' exposition is most sound. His grasp of the Apostle's thought is so firm, his manner of setting it forth so lucid, that we should be surprised if any one could read this book and not feel that he understands St. Paul's Gospel better than before."—*Scotsman.*

"Dr. Dykes' language is always dignified and felicitous, his exposition of truth lucid and forcible, his teaching valuable, and above all there is in everything he writes a warm ethical glow which communicates itself to the reader. Dr. Dykes deserves the gratitude of readers of the New Testament for his clear and animated explanation."—*British Weekly.*

THE SABBATICAL REST OF GOD AND MAN: A Study on Hebrews IV. 3, 9. By the Rev. JOHN HUGHES, M.A. 7s. 6d.

"This volume is the result of a careful and intelligent study of all the literature of the subject, and has been made in a fresh and suggestive way."—*Liverpool Mercury.*

"An able and eloquent exposition."—*Literary World.*

LANDMARKS OF NEW TESTAMENT MORALITY. By the Rev. GEORGE MATHESON, D.D. 6s.

"For originality of treatment, firm grasp of the points of likeness and difference between Christian and heathen systems of morality, and clearness of style, we can speak in terms of commendation of this volume."—*Guardian.*

"The book is emphatically an interesting one for thoughtful readers, and suggestive of divers trains of meditation which might well be followed out in further detail."—*Record.*

"The book, as a whole, is marked by the high qualities we are accustomed to find in Dr. Matheson's writings. It is able, fresh, suggestive, and distinguished by cogency of reasoning and clearness and breadth of style."—*Scots Observer.*

THE CHRISTIAN FULFILMENTS AND USES OF THE LEVITICAL SIN-OFFERING. By the Rev. HENRY BATCHELOR. 5s.

"Mr. Batchelor puts with clearness and cogency the argument from the Levitical usage."—*British Weekly.*

"This is a treatise in which we know not whether to admire more the ability or the soundness of the author. As the second is the rarer quality just now, we award it our highest praise. Mr. Batchelor is altogether with us in the battle of the 'Down-Grade.'"—Mr. SPURGEON in the *Sword and Trowel.*

"A scholarly, compact, clear, forcible, and fervent defence of the orthodox substitutionary view of the Atonement."—*Nonconformist.*

CHRISTIANITY AND EVOLUTION ; or, Modern Problems of the Faith. By various Writers. 6s.

"Each writer takes up a distinct side of the subject, and treats it always intelligently, sometimes with really striking ability and acuteness."—*Literary Churchman.*

"These papers are, on the whole, unusually able and earnest."—*Methodist Times.*

"The variety in the standpoints of the writers renders the results of their inquiries the more valuable to earnest seekers after the truth. We can heartily recommend the book."—*Church Bells.*

NON-BIBLICAL SYSTEMS OF RELIGION : A Symposium. By various Writers. 6s.

"A volume which will be welcome to students of Comparative Religion. The papers give a comprehensive view of the various beliefs which had allegiance from man before the dawn of Christianity, and give such an account of them as any but a special student will find at once profitable and enjoyable."—*Scotsman.*

"This is essentially a book for the day. Altogether the volume supplies much valuable information, and is suggestive of further inquiry to thoughtful students."—*Church Bells.*

THE MENTAL CHARACTERISTICS OF OUR LORD. By the Rev. H. N. BERNARD, M.A. 6s.

"A very interesting volume. The subject is of supreme importance, and the treatment is not only agreeable but thoughtful."—*Church Bells.*

"We have read the book with interest and profit, and the ninth chapter, 'On the Prayers of the Lord Jesus Christ,' is really very valuable."—*Record.*

INSPIRATION : A Symposium on In what Sense and within what Limits is the Bible the Word of God? By the Ven. Archdeacon FARRAR, the Revs. Principal CAIRNS, Professor STANLEY LEATHES, D.D., Prebendary ROW, and others. 6s.

"The volume is an interesting one, written throughout in a temperate and scholarly spirit, and likely to prove useful to the higher stamp of theological students."—*Church Times.*

IMMORTALITY: A Symposium on What are the Foundations of the Belief in the Immortality of Man? By the Rev. Prebendary Row, M.A., Rabbi HERMANN ADLER, Professor G. G. STOKES, F.R.S., Rev. Canon KNOX-LITTLE, Rev. EDWARD WHITE, and others. 6s.

"The volume is full of interest and suggestiveness."—*British Quarterly Review.*

"A work of great and absorbing interest, marked by extreme ability."—*Literary Churchman.*

THE PATRIARCHAL TIMES. By the Rev. THOMAS WHITELAW, D.D. 6s.

"The essays form individually and as a whole an articulated chain of reasoning, the charm of which consists in the fact, that having presented to the reader a convincing conclusion, it leaves him in a state of wonder that he had never arrived there on his own account."—*Record.*

FUTURE PROBATION: A Symposium on the Question, "Is Salvation Possible after Death?" By the Rev. STANLEY LEATHES, D.D., Principal J. CAIRNS, D.D., LL.D., Rev. EDWARD WHITE, Rev. STOPFORD BROOKE, M.A., Rev. Dr. LITTLEDALE, Right Rev. the BISHOP of AMYCLA, &c. 6s.

"This volume deals with a subject of profound and awful moment, and the papers as a whole are written with considerable ability."—*Literary Churchman.*

"To men affected with the 'malady of thought' this book will prove delightful reading; and to men not so affected, we hope it will carry the infection."—*Irish Ecclesiastical Gazette.*

FOUR CENTURIES OF SILENCE; or, From Malachi to Christ. By the Rev. R. A. REDFORD, M.A., LL.B., Professor of Systematic Theology and Apologetics, New College, London. 6s.

"Carefully and intelligently done. The critical views expressed appear to us generally just. His account of Philo is particularly good."—*Literary Churchman.*

"It would be difficult to speak too highly of the wide reading, the careful and discriminating thought, and the wise and cautious judgments by which, throughout, the work is characterised. Every chapter is full of most interesting information and discussion."—*British Quarterly Review.*

THE FIRST LETTER OF PAUL THE APOSTLE TO TIMOTHY. A Popular Commentary. With a Series of Forty Sermonettes. By ALFRED ROWLAND, LL.B., B.A. 6s.

"We have here a series of notes derived from the best authorities, and put in a shape that makes them intelligible to mere English readers. . . . The sermons are decidedly on a high level, well thought out, well expressed, and every way effective and useful."—*Church Bells.*

"Every important passage of the Epistle is handled in turn with earnestness and good sense. The discourses are enriched with apposite quotation and sound exposition."—*London Quarterly Review.*

THE FIRST EPISTLE OF ST. JOHN: An Exposition with Homiletical Treatment. By the Rev. J. J. LIAS, M.A. 7s. 6d.

"We cannot speak too highly of this volume. It is full of sober piety, guided by sound scholarship; and Mr. Lias seems to have acquired, from his long study of St. John's writings, something of the Apostle's marvellous power of using such language as is simple and intelligible to the plainest folk, while at the same time it expresses the deepest thoughts and suggests reflections upon which the noblest intellects may worthily exercise their highest powers."—*Church Quarterly Review.*

"We can say quite confidently that we know of no other Commentary on this Epistle which is to be preferred to this, and hardly any worthy to rank beside it."—*John Bull.*

"One of the most beautiful, instructive, and edifying expositions of St. John's First Epistle we have ever seen. Mr. Lias seems to us to have entered into the very heart of St. John's Divine Theology. We know of no book that throws more light upon the teaching of the Apostle whom Jesus loved. It responds to some of the holiest aspirations of the Christian soul."—*Methodist Times.*

"The work is of the highest order, and ought to be in the hands of any one who really desires to understand this part of the Scriptures."—*Aberdeen Free Press.*

DANIEL I.-VI.: An Exposition of the Historical Portion of the Writings of the Prophet Daniel. By the Very Rev. R. PAYNE SMITH, D.D., Dean of Canterbury. 6s.

"These papers are of sterling value, and cover much ground that is imperfectly known, or not known at all. No one could possibly read the volume without adding greatly to their knowledge of this important prophecy."—*Literary Churchman.*

"These papers are full of moral and spiritual application of the numerous instructive points in the histories dealt with. They contain much information drawn from modern discoveries, proving the authenticity and illustrating the details of Daniel's narratives."—*Record.*

ZECHARIAH: His Visions and his Warnings. By W. LINDSAY ALEXANDER, D.D. 6s.

"Those who have found difficulty in grasping the brief and mysterious parables of the Hebrew Prophet will derive great help in their study of this prophecy from Dr. Alexander's careful and painstaking discussion."—*Literary Churchman.*

"As we pass from chapter to chapter of the Commentary, we are impressed with the spiritual insight and the moral and intellectual force of the writer. Take, for example, the chapter on the Candelabrum and the Olive Trees, and one gains from the exposition an amount of historical, linguistic, and spiritual instruction which could hardly have been expected. For those who are studying the Hebrew Scriptures in the original there is much help. The exposition of the Prophet's meaning in reference to his own age is sober and sound; and the bearing of the writing upon the Church of God in all ages, and the spiritual import of the imagery and the history, are excellently brought out and illustrated."—*Church Bells.*

LONDON: JAMES NISBET & CO., 21 BERNERS STREET.

www.ingramcontent.com/pod-product-compliance
Lightning Source LLC
Chambersburg PA
CBHW020812230426
43666CB00007B/974